Praise for *Libe*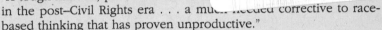

An *Amazon* "recommended book":
"A tough-minded, provocative indict~~~~~~~~~~~~~~~~~~~~~~~~~~
in the post–Civil Rights era . . . a mu~~~~~~~~~~ corrective to race-based thinking that has proven unproductive."
—David Nicholson, Black Studies and Literature Editor of *Amazon*

"Before President Clinton's national conversation on race goes any further, he should take the time to read this important contribution."
—Richard D. Kahlenberg, author of *The Remedy: Class, Race, and Affirmative Action*

"Sleeper doesn't sneer; he argues skillfully and persuasively. And he takes pains to make *Liberal Racism* a critique of the left, not an endorsement of the right. . . . If he is particularly disappointed in liberals, Sleeper tells us, it is only because he expects more of them in the first place."
—Eric Liu, *The Washington Post*

"In this short, highly accessible and often insightful book, Sleeper scores several strong points: . . . the liberal left has always been compelled to use race instead of class to bring about social change and has become trapped in this strategy by a combination of genuine puritanical moralism about racism and sheer political opportunism."
—Gerald Early, *Chicago Tribune*

"To truly inspire a new dialogue on race, President Clinton will need to push further. Jim Sleeper frames the challenge well: 'Our best leaders are those who show their neighbors, every day, how to leave subgroup loyalties behind at the doors of classrooms, jury rooms, hiring halls . . .' That's far better advice than anything Clinton's advisory panel has offered so far."
—Ronald Brownstein, national correspondent, *Los Angeles Times*

"Jim Sleeper's provocative confrontation with liberal ideology is no defense of the conservative approach to race. Rather he challenges liberals, who once fought to help America rise above color, to get back to their abandoned program of a transracial civic faith. Read *Liberal Racism* and then, if you dare, take a long look in the mirror."
—C. Eric Lincoln, Duke University, author of *The Black Muslim in America* and *The Black Church in the African-American Experience*

"If race is a concept with dubious biological and philosophical foundations, why continue to validate it? Why not argue, as Sleeper has done, for a more nuanced accommodation and celebration of *ethnic* differences and abandon the theoretical construct race and its destructive corollary, racism?"
—Mary Lefkowitz, *The New York Times*, author of *Not Out of Africa*

"A lot of us would agree with Sleeper that if you scratch through the surface of skin color, you will find a good deal of common morality— mostly based on the primacy of individual character and integrity."
—William Raspberry, *The Washington Post*

"Like a Toto in Oz, Jim Sleeper has made his mark lifting the curtain on liberal racism's inconsistencies and hypocrisies. Sleeper's discerning eye details a host of political absurdities, and his lucid prose is a pleasure to read."
—Salim Muwakkil, *Newsday*

"Jim Sleeper has written an important book that deserves to be read and carefully considered, especially if Americans are going to engage fruitfully in that 'national conversation' about race that President Bill Clinton has promised. Sleeper's essays on black identity and what he contends is our lost civic culture are particularly strong, especially the chapter focusing on Harvard Law Prof. Randall Kennedy and Boston University economist Glenn Loury, two of the most thoughtful and intriguing black intellectuals in the nation today."
—Don Wycliff, *Commonweal*

"Sleeper will be called a whiner, a bellyacher, even a racist. Of course, of course. But he is a liberal whose knee does not jerk. He has been examining liberals' rejection of a common American civic culture for several years, but nothing he has written is as candid as what he gives us here. . . . These are words liberals need to hear. They need to hear them because they are true."
—Michael Skube, *The Atlanta Journal-Constitution*

"To read this frequently brilliant book is to realize just how far we have gone toward exalting race and racial differences as the dominant realities of our civic life. Sleeper's strict and sweeping definition of liberal racism catches many of us—Democrats and Republicans alike—in its net."
—Chris Tucker, *The Dallas Morning News*

PENGUIN BOOKS

LIBERAL RACISM

Jim Sleeper, the veteran columnist and essayist, writes on civic culture and racial politics. Former political columnist for the New York *Daily News* and author of *The Closest of Strangers*, he has written for *Harper's*, *The New Republic*, *The New Yorker*, *The Nation*, *Washington Monthly*, and *Dissent*. A graduate of Yale with a doctorate in education from Harvard, he lives in New York City.

LIBERAL
R A C I S M

JIM SLEEPER

PENGUIN BOOKS

PENGUIN BOOKS

Published by the Penguin Group
Penguin Putnam Inc., 375 Hudson Street,
New York, New York 10014, U.S.A.
Penguin Books Ltd, 27 Wrights Lane,
London W8 5TZ, England
Penguin Books Australia Ltd, Ringwood,
Victoria, Australia
Penguin Books Canada Ltd, 10 Alcorn Avenue,
Toronto, Ontario, Canada M4V 3B2
Penguin Books (N.Z.) Ltd, 182–190 Wairau Road,
Auckland 10, New Zealand
Penguin India, 210 Chiranjiv Tower, 43 Nehru Place,
New Delhi 11009, India

Penguin Books Ltd, Registered Offices:
Harmondsworth, Middlesex, England

First published in the United States of America by Viking Penguin,
a member of Penguin Putnam Inc. 1997
Published in Penguin Books 1998

1 3 5 7 9 10 8 6 4 2

Grateful acknowledgment is made for permission to reprint
excerpts from the following copyrighted works:
W. E. B. DuBois: Biography of a Race, 1868–1919 by David Levering Lewis
(Henry Holt). By permission of the author.
"Junior and John Doe" by James A. McPherson. First appeared in Lure and
Loathing: Essays on Race, Identity, and the Ambivalence of Assimilation edited
by Gerald Early, Penguin Books. Copyright © James A. McPherson, 1993.
By permission of the author. "On Becoming an American Writer" by James A.
McPherson. First appeared in the Atlantic Monthly, December 1978.
By permission of the author.
Out of America: A Black Man Confronts Africa by Keith B. Richburg. Copyright
© 1997 by Keith B. Richburg. By permission of HarperCollins Publishers Inc.

ISBN 0-670-87391-8 (hc.)
ISBN 0 14 02.6378 0 (pbk.)
(CIP data available)

Printed in the United States of America
Set in ITC Garamond Light
Designed by Levavi & Levavi

For Arnold J. Sleeper and Fredelle G. Sleeper,
who taught me to look past appearances.

Acknowledgments

A grateful author often names those "without whom this book could not have been written" and then hastens to exonerate them ("Any faults in these pages are mine alone"), sometimes even while seeking a bit of insulation by invoking their names. I *am* deeply grateful to many people, but rather than implicate them in this broadside, I have thanked them personally, some of them in ways I'm sure they won't forget.

I do want to thank here some smart professionals who did the actual "heavy lifting" to bring out this book. It simply wouldn't exist without astute research by Mark Oppenheimer, one of the most promising young writers I have known, and by Peter Edelman, a senior librarian at the New York *Daily News*. My marvelous agent, Virginia Barber, and her associate, Jay Mandel, were hard bargainers, gentle hand-holders, and careful readers all the way. At Viking Penguin, executive director Cathy Hemming, manuscript editor Marion Maneker, editorial assistants Molly Stern and Erin Boyle, copyeditors Barbara Campo and Cathy Dexter, and others made up a wonderfully effective publishing team.

CONTENTS

CHAPTER I

LIFE AFTER DIVERSITY

◆ **The Liberal Default**

Students now enter college with their group identities intact, and they expect the institution to respond accordingly. . . . People have come to identify themselves not only according to race, gender, or ethnic identity, but also by class, sexual orientation, disability, and age.

—Edgar Beckham,
vice president,
Ford Foundation

When I was a senior at the Bronx High School of Science, Harvard's admissions materials showed up in my mailbox, unsolicited. Out came this Minority Student Information Request Card and a leaflet saying, "Here are some of the things Hispanic students experience at Harvard." And I thought, "What is this? I want to know, what do students experience at Harvard? Like, what am I to them?" Well, I knew what I was. I was the fulfillment of a quota. And I have no intention of being that.

—Rafael Olmeda, reporter,
New York *Daily News*

Edgar Beckham's assumption that your skin color signals a "group identity" is now liberal doctrine. It drives the color-coding of American public policy and civic culture, and it is a colossal blunder. Rafael Olmeda is proud of his Puerto Rican heritage, he has known the discrimination and bigotry to which the term "racist" usually applies, and he accepts limited affirmative action as a remedy for discrimination. A busy young reporter at an urban tabloid newspaper, Olmeda doesn't read conservative tracts or magazines. But he feels patronized and insulted by liberal racial solicitude far more often than he feels oppressed by the conservative racism that dominates the liberal imagination. "When I face people in a newsroom or the street, I don't want them assuming they know anything important about me because of my name or my color," Olmeda says. "They have no right to do that."

Many of today's liberals assume that right. They have been trying to color-code Olmeda's sense of himself and his country since long before he felt put off by Harvard's approach to him as a colored person. Claiming to oppose historic racism, the liberal "diversity" project defaults on America's promise, sometimes by reinforcing racial "awareness" on campus and on the job in ways even segregationists might applaud. Constraining us all to define our citizenship and even our personhood more and more by race and ethnicity in classrooms, workrooms, courtrooms, newsrooms, and boardrooms, today's liberalism no longer curbs discrimination; it invites it. It does not expose racism; it recapitulates and, sometimes, reinvents it. Its tortured racial etiquette begets racial epithets, as surely as hypocrisy begets hostility. And it dishonors liberals' own heroic past efforts to focus America's race lens in the 1950s and '60s, when conservative pieties about color blindness concealed monstrous injustices.

Liberals who still challenge such injustices are right to argue that sometimes only the power of law, vigorously enforced, can block racial discrimination. They are right to insist that blacks, Native Americans, and many Hispanics, incorporated involuntarily into the American experiment, have some special claims on public institutions—the very courts, legislatures, and schools that worked so long to degrade them. They are right to remind us that, given half a chance, the rich will grind the faces of the poor and need occasionally to be restrained and taught decency by the rest of us. But these truths do not offset the bitter irony that many liberals who fought nobly to help this country rise above color have become so blinded by color that they have leapt ahead of conservatives to draw new race lines in the civic sand. Conservatives may have gotten race wrong, but that does not mean that liberals have gotten it right, and we are well past the time when liberals can point fingers at racist and capitalist bogeymen across the ideological divide to justify their own abandonment of a transracial belonging and civic faith for which Americans of all colors so obviously yearn.

In this book I recount how liberals have lost that faith, letting down their fellow citizens of all colors even while claiming to assail racism. I describe the civic balance we need to reclaim in our public life if we are to undo the damage that liberal myopia has done. I think I speak for many other Americans who are uncomfortable around the ideologically or racially encamped, whether on the left or on the right, and whether in distinct groupings of blacks, Hispanics, Asians, or whites. If we could truly eliminate racism from our national life, neither conservatives nor liberals would emerge covered with glory. But I emphasize the liberal default in these pages because it has been so unexpected and—given liberalism's promises—so fateful.

◆

It was Congressman Major Owens, a black representative from New York City, who in 1981 first told me and other members of a small audience of liberal activists and journalists that "liberals are sometimes the worst racists." Mystified though I was by that remark, I knew it was no polemical flourish; Owens, a child of the South and a graduate of the proud, black Morehouse College, had forged strong ties to white liberals in the 1950s on his way to becoming a librarian and activist in Brooklyn. Still, it took me a few years to understand what he meant. Perhaps this book can save other liberals some time.

Only gradually did I realize that liberal racism has several dimensions. Sometimes, prompted by misdirected and self-congratulatory compassion, liberal racism patronizes nonwhites by expecting (and getting) less of them than they are fully capable of achieving. Intending to turn the tables on racist double standards that set the bar much higher for nonwhites, liberal racism ends up perpetuating double standards by setting the bar so much lower for its intended beneficiaries that it denies them the satisfactions of equal accomplishment and opportunity.

Liberal racism also assumes that racial differences are so profound that they are almost primordial. The term "racialism" is sometimes used to denote this belief that racial differences are essential to our understandings of ourselves and society, and at times I will use it to refer to such thinking. But the fascination with racial differences that prevents many liberals from treating any person with a nonwhite racial physiognomy as someone much like themselves only begets policies and programs that reinforce nineteenth-century assumptions about race that are patently racist. It is time to call this mindset what it is: liberal racism.

Yet another dimension is the visceral discomfort some white liberals feel with nonwhites. Some white liberals, insulated from honest give-and-take with blacks and hobbled by guilt and fear of the unknown, seem so wary of such encounters that they construct intricate latticeworks of racial rectitude and noble stereotypes to mask their own fears. Their compensatory, fervent gestures of goodwill are sometimes amusing, often just sad. And some blacks—especially irresponsible leaders and public poseurs who appear in these pages—have learned to "play" liberal avoidance strategies for all they're worth.

Since liberals often argue that other people's racism is all the more dangerous for being unconscious, one might expect them to be the first to suspect and uncover their own. But instead of uncovering it, liberal institutions such as the Ford and other foundations fund it; activists and politicians pander to it; and the *New York Times* and other media disseminate its view of the world. Liberals who assume that one's skin color is one's destiny tend to deceive themselves and others about that belief. They behave remarkably like "quality white folks" in the old South, who condescended sweetly to blacks while projecting contempt for inferiors onto poor whites and onto blacks who chose not to be charmed by elite gestures of affection. Today's liberal racists are more willing, even eager, to accept black criticism—as long as it is ritualized and therefore exculpatory, and somewhat entertaining. Such liberals applaud society's thirty-year-long regression from trying in the 1960s to ensure that people were not categorized officially by color and surname to ensuring now that they are so categorized, at liberals' own behest.

One could call all this "friendly racism," but its apparent solicitude yields few friendships and little mutual respect. The "antiracist" protocols that liberal racists impose upon public-school teachers, bureaucrats, and corporate chief executive officers have become so emptied of meaning that those who follow them trade mainly on petty or fabricated resentments, which fester as proxies for real problems that remain unaddressed. As I will show in the next chapter, on perceptions of crime, liberals often think that they can treat any black skin as an automatic signifier of disadvantage and aggrievement; yet they are shocked when urban police officers and taxidrivers—many of them black—treat blackness the same way, treating blacks as bearers of deficiency and anger who are not full citizens and legitimate customers. As I show in Chapter 3, on voting rights, liberals seem to think that they can integrate legislatures more fully by segregating voters racially. Chapter 4, on media, shows how liberal journalists sometimes compound such problems by reporting news in the language of racial groupthink, applying different standards to people of different colors—in the name, ironically, of "inclusion."

Not only are such liberal strategies racist; as Americans' understandings of race become more fluid and ecumenical, the strategies seem ridiculous. When an Irish-American family tried to adopt a black baby abandoned in a Brooklyn hospital, liberals saw a threat to black integrity: The family was told that state regulations imposed at the behest of the National Association of Black Social Workers mandated a "culturally consistent" (i.e., same-race) environment for the child—even if that meant that the baby must languish for months in the hospital until a suitable black family could be found. At a hospital meeting for prospective parents, the father of the white would-be adoptive family protested. "All of the thirty other people at the meeting were black or Latino," he recalls. "These people, not an ideologue among them, agreed with me loudly: 'What kind of nonsense is this?' The social worker was sympathetic but said the regulations came from the state."

Like these parents of all colors who supported the would-be adoptive white family, millions of liberal racism's intended beneficiaries are disdained or distrusted when they reach "inappropriately" across color lines. Yet such open-minded people are our future, and if they now are voiceless, it is only because they are leaderless. Liberal racism has gotten their priorities and aspirations backward by insisting that more institutional "respect" for racial identity would enhance individual dignity. This is no longer simply a misconception; it is a lie. Beneath liberal racists' institutional radar, a new American identity is being forged, and, with good leadership, it will spawn a rebellion that sends liberal "diversity" doctrine off into the past with Chairman Mao Zedong's "Little Red Book," whose prescriptions for Third World socialism some multiculturalist advocates, teachers, consultants, and journalists used to take as seriously as they do racialist nonsense now.

Since the story of liberal racism is not one of conspiracy but of folly, this book must track a mind-set that barely knows itself, in a country that knows itself little better. After describing liberal racism's colorization of perceptions of crime, of voting rights, and of the news media in the next three chapters, we leave such horror stories aside to explore in Chapter 5 some mysteries of black identity that have deepened amid growing confusion about American identity and the classical liberal principles upon which black progress so fatefully depends. In Chapter 6, we share in the cogitations and soul-searching of two black thinkers who have wrestled with liberal assumptions about race, one moving from the left toward the center of our national experiment, the other moving toward it from the right. In Chapter 7, we consider what we might salvage from the best of American civic culture, which liberals abandoned on the assumption that it was inherently and inevitably racist. First, let me establish a few principles to guide us on our journey.

◆ Liberals' Lost Mission

This book's premise is that precisely because the United States is becoming racially, ethnically, and religiously more complex than institutional color-coding can comprehend, liberals should be working overtime to nurture some shared American principles and bonds that strengthen national belonging and nourish democratic habits. Alone among the nations, such as France and the Soviet Union, that have made globe-girdling, universal claims, the American nation abducted and plunged into its "white" midst millions of black people who, in consequence, had the highest possible stakes in the country's fulfillment of its oft-stated creed. This gives us opportunities and challenges unprecedented in human history. By the accidents of history and the irrepressible logic of the founders' intent, it is America's destiny to show the world how to eliminate racial differences—culturally, morally, and even physically—as factors in human striving.

Liberals should herald this truth, not shrink from it, as they so often do now. They should champion a common civic culture that is strong enough to balance parochialism with universalism, and deep enough to sustain individual freedom amid a robust sense of obligation to the common good. They should teach every American who enters a jury room, teaches a class, or reports a news story to make it a point of pride to mute and even abandon his or her racial affinities in order to stand, at least briefly, for the whole. That is possible only if

American civic culture and identity are "thick" enough to live in on race-transcendent terms. Liberals should be weaving that thick social fabric.

Since early in this century, liberals have been the great framers of race-transcending American public narratives that struck the right balances between parochialism and universalism and between individual autonomy and communal obligation. Liberals dared and helped people of all colors to rise above whatever was keeping them isolated and small. The socialist labor leader Eugene Victor Debs did that; the two presidents Roosevelt did it; even the Communists of the Popular Front in the 1930s did it, albeit for reasons that few now care to defend. Today's liberals have abandoned all national moral storytelling to conservatives because they are afraid to take the lead in wresting our racial discourse from ethnocentric activists as well as white supremacists, from the left as well as the right—and, yes, from blacks as well as whites.

Why are so many liberals toeing the color line instead of crossing it or even trampling it? The most obvious reason is that liberals remain sensitive to the fact that black and white Americans have been locked in a three-centuries-old physical and psychic embrace. That embrace was as intimate as it was miserable, and, even now, as it loosens, fears as well as hopes are stirring the hearts of the newly disentangled. Many just aren't ready to let go, because they long ago let the terms of past racial encounters define what they are. "Few of us would choose to be rendered raceless—to be suddenly without a tribe," writes the black journalist Ellis Cose. But the stark truth is that neither whiteness nor blackness in America harbors any lasting cultural meanings, apart from the ones imposed and sometimes lovingly embellished under segregation. From the black Baptist and Methodist churches to the blues and jazz, black culture has been a treasure chest of survival tools—the finest ever created in America. But as the terms of survival change, so must the tools. Liberals, black as well as white, are shrinking from their obligation to acknowledge this. Apparently they cannot bear to learn that when blackness and whiteness are no longer locked together, neither can define itself clearly enough to serve as a vessel of hope.

Liberals often try to justify their fixation on color by citing Supreme Court Justice Harry Blackmun's wise dictum in the *Bakke* affirmative-action case: "In order to get beyond racism, we must first take account of race. There is no other way. And in order to treat some persons equally, we must treat them differently." It was in that hopeful spirit that liberals first imposed racial remedies upon settled civic and communal arrangements, from election districting to neighborhood schooling. But that is not the spirit in which they have continued to color-code our public and private lives. The new spirit is one of fatalism. They give no sign of wanting truly to "get beyond racism."

Blackmun's claim that we must "first take account of race" (he might better have written that we must *sometimes* or *temporarily* take account of it) should make us ask whether and when it is still useful to racialize civic interactions. Sometimes it is; often it is not. Liberals' refusal or inability to draw that distinction has cost them political credibility and power. Edgar Beckham's claim that students enter college with racial and other group identities "intact" and that institutions should be configured to "respond accordingly" is as far from Blackmun's dictum as one can get. Yet Beckham's is a succinct statement of today's liberal folly.

So deeply are liberals in denial about this default that the moment the conservative "revolution" of 1994 began to falter on its own hypocrisies and inherent contradictions, they predicted that, reincarnated as "progressives," they would win back enough power in the 1996 elections to curb economic injustice and racial division. Instead, as I will show in Chapter 3, some of the returns suggested that liberals, under whatever name, will never sustain a governing agenda that has broad public support until they reckon more deeply with how they have gotten race wrong. Liberals can always gain some electoral ground by capitalizing on conservatives' lies and blunders, as conservatives have capitalized on theirs—with facile repositionings toward the "center" and with tit-for-tat scandal-mongering and scare tactics. But unless liberals come clean about their own racism, nothing will come of all their finger-pointing at others' bigotry.

Absent such a reckoning, many Americans have actually had to outfox liberals to advance racial justice. In the 1996 elections, for example, hundreds of thousands of moderate white voters in white-majority congressional districts in the South elected black incumbents who had come seeking their support. These voters were able to rebut the presumption that they were racists only because, prior to the election, a conservative Supreme Court majority, ignoring liberal prophecies of racial doom, invalidated the establishment of racially determined congressional districts drawn by liberals (with help from cynical conservative Republican operatives) who had insisted that fair-minded white majorities simply didn't exist.

Liberals have defaulted in such controversies partly because they have lost touch with, and faith in, civil society—the web of voluntary associations in families, churches, neighborhood groups, and civic, educational, and labor organizations where democratic dispositions are nourished and given practical scope. The early civil rights movement knew better. It won what most Americans recognized as justice by affirming that even a flawed civil society should be embraced and redeemed, not deconstructed and micromanaged as inherently, eternally racist. Practicing a politics of persuasion that distinguishes this country from Serbia, Rwanda, and even France, the movement made canny but resonant appeals to "angry white men's" decency, even as it exposed their shortcomings. It understood that while this is a nation of laws, ultimately it is more than a courtroom. Today's liberals have forgotten that law works best when it is introduced deftly, on the cusp of a civic consensus nourished by the politics of persuasion and not by assumptions that everyone is operating in bad faith.

So deep is the liberal default that Barry Goldwater has become a better friend of racial integration than Benjamin Chavis Muhammad, the former president of the National Association for the Advancement of Colored People who has joined the Nation of Islam, and Newt Gingrich is less prone to exploiting racial fears and resentments than is Congress-woman Maxine Waters of South-Central Los Angeles. When it comes to race some conservatives *are* more "progressive" than liberals.

◆ Wrinkles on the Right

But only some. Many conservatives hypocritically praise civil society as an antidote to the bureaucratic state, even as they champion market forces that disrupt and erode traditional American networks of sharing and trust. For all their celebrations of color blindness and their testimony that in a free-market society the only important color is green, many conservatives' notions about race seem to doom them to spin and subsidize geneticist propositions about black inadequacy and pathology. Time and again they find themselves beating embarrassed retreats from such obviously un-American stuff and from the cynical, "wedge-issue" politics that divides people by color.

But liberal racism also divides people that way, and there is no better proof than in the support or indulgence it gets from opportunistic conservatives. Liberal "voting rights" activists cannot explain why their race-based election redistricting proposals have been backed by conservative foundations and Republican operatives, or why their notions of racial "identity" and "diversity" are embraced and even inculcated by the nation's meanest, leanest corporations. But it really isn't a mystery. Since the law in a classical liberal capitalist society responds better to claims of racial discrimination than to claims of economic abuse, liberals have gone to court over race, not economic class. Imperative though it was to secure civil rights that way, the liberal strategy has become a permanent evasion of liberals' true moral and intellectual responsibility—recognized by Adam Smith and John Stuart Mill—to set reasonable limits on free markets that erode civic virtue. Color-coding is cheaper than trust-busting or denouncing Time-Warner for promoting gangsta rap, but color-coding is no better a solution to racism than is a conservatism that occasionally tries to put markets in their place. Liberal racism thwarts a transracial, class politics that could seriously challenge abuses of economic power, and there is no clear evidence that most liberals are up to making that challenge. And racism eclipses the American identity and national narratives that once gave such class politics some traction.

Conservative racial ideas and initiatives do sometimes serve as necessary correctives to ghastly liberal blunders that might otherwise have remained unacknowledged and unstopped. Conservatives also have important lessons to teach the left about markets, which sometimes stimulate civic virtue by throwing people together across old lines of racial enmity, confounding ancient superstitions and feuds. Fifteen years ago, the writer Susan Sontag told a shocked audience of fellow leftist-liberals that the relatively conservative *Reader's Digest* had long been a better guide to the Cold War than the leftist weekly *The Nation*. Certainly the *Digest* was more accurate and morally right about Communism, but Sontag didn't mean that just because it sounded alarms about Communism, it was therefore Americans' best guide to democratic foreign policy making. Nor are conservatives our best guides to rejuvenating civic culture now, even when they're right about the absurdities of liberal racism.

To its great glory and unending consternation, the United States will remain a capitalist country, and the question is whether liberals can temper its excesses more wisely than by subdividing it into imagined racial "cultures" (African American, European American, Hispanic American, Asian American, and Native American), a scheme that hobbles good pedagogy, politics, and public policy. The best of the civic culture which the early civil rights movement tried to embrace and redeem presumes not that our racial and ethnic story lines and affinities should disappear, but that they should not prevail as the central organizing principles of our public life. Yet some liberals support racial remedies as sops to their own consciences, perhaps because they are complicit in a flawed liberal capitalism which they do not actually oppose yet cannot quite bring themselves to defend. They support such remedies because they have no serious intention of redressing deeper inequities that divide not only whites from blacks but also whites from whites (and, increasingly, blacks from blacks).

◆ Americanism and Universalism

Liberals have lost touch with the basic principles of classical liberalism itself. No movement for social justice can make headway in a pluralist society without keeping classical liberal commitments to rational analysis—to the primacy of often provisional and evolving public truths over the mythic, communal ones that are enshrouded in racial narratives. Nor is justice possible without a commitment to individual over group rights in a context of civil and moral obligation to other individuals across race lines—the right, for example, to dissent from or to leave one's own subculture without fear. Without a working faith in such principles, movements and societies sink into a tribalism whose brutality is all too well known.

Necessary as they are, the classical liberal commitments are still insufficient. People who stake everything on them find themselves soaring into universalisms so removed from human reality that they end up creating holy inquisitions or gulags. We need a better way. And there is one. It involves the American civic cultural genius for tempering the universal with the parochial, without succumbing to the tribal. Liberal constitutional democracy and the civil society that sustains it aren't perfect, but they embody historic human gains that more ambitious revolutionaries have repealed only at great cost. As a self-conscious social experiment, the United States is the only multiracial civilization to nourish the seeds of its own transcendence. People of all colors, believing this, have watered those seeds with their blood and tears. Yet liberal educators no longer show young Americans how to think of such people as their own forebears whatever their race, and how to keep faith with their legacy.

The costs of such pedagogy are evident not in the number

of people who actually believe it, but in the extent to which it distracts or prevents them from helping the American promise to come true. They are left confused and impotent before the more brutal turns which "identity politics" often takes on urban streets and in hard-pressed rural areas. Perhaps the only thing that inner-city gangs, white militias, and the Nation of Islam have in common is thousands of young men bereft of an American civic culture that is potent enough to draw them into rites of passage that would make them all they can be—and reward them credibly for becoming it. Hence the invasion of the public square by Louis Farrakhan and Snoop Doggy Dog, by Pat Robertson and Timothy Mc-Veigh—all disowning one another but all "united" in being marketed by political and media producers who profit handsomely from sensationalizing their assaults. "Fundamentalists rush in where liberals fear to tread," warns the political philosopher Michael Sandel. Liberal racism is no answer to these fundamentalisms; it is a capitulation to them.

But just as liberals will get nowhere by obsessing about white malevolence, malingering, and myopia, they will fail in their mission, as conservatives have, if they profess color blindness too sweepingly and too soon. The challenge we all must face is the mystery at the center of American black identity, especially, that has been exposed by the vacuum at the center of classical liberalism itself.

◆ An American Mystery

Early in 1997 I happened upon a C-Span telecast of the awarding of seven Congressional Medals of Honor to black World War II veterans, each of whose "gallantry and intrepidity at the risk of his life" had been ignored for more than fifty years. President Clinton strode across the East Room of the White House to present the medals to Vernon Joseph Baker, at seventy-seven the only recipient still living, and to the families of the others. "History has been made whole today," the president told the assembly, adding that the honorees had "helped us find a way to become a more just, more free nation . . . more worthy of them and true to its ideals."

History has not been made whole for American blacks, of course, and yet something almost archaic in the recipients' bearing and in the ceremony itself reminded me that none of us in the younger generations can say with certainty what an American wholeness might be, or, within it, what blackness or whiteness might mean. If we have trouble thinking about race, it's because we no longer know how to think about America itself.

At least Second Lieutenant Baker seemed to have less trouble half a century ago than we do now. In April 1945, he single-handedly wiped out two German machine-gun nests in Viareggio, Italy; drew fire on himself to permit the evacuation of wounded comrades; and led his segregated battalion's advance through enemy minefields. Asked by reporters after the East Room ceremony whether he had ever given up hope of winning the medal, he "sounded surprised . . . as if the question presumed arrogance," the *New York Times* reported. "I never thought about getting it," Baker said. Asked why he had joined the army in the first place, he responded, "Well, I was a young black man without a job."

Ah, yes, *that*. Prodded to comment on having risked his life for his country while in a segregated unit, he answered, "I was an angry young man; we were all angry, but we had a job to do, and we did it. . . . My personal thoughts were that I knew things would get better, and I'm happy I'm here to see it." Anyone might be happy if, after fighting in a segregated black unit, he lived to see a black chairman of the Joint Chiefs of Staff. But, of course, that isn't all Baker has seen, for "intrepidity" like his is often eclipsed now by that of young black Americans killing one another. When he said, "I knew things would get better," perhaps he was measuring his words for the occasion.

Asked what the ceremony meant to her, Arlene Fox, widow of First Lieutenant John Fox, who died in Italy in 1944, said, "I think it's more than just what it means to this family. I think it sends a message . . . that when a man does his duty, his color isn't important." Perhaps she, too, was measuring her words.

Yet I think not. Even in the prime of their anger, Vernon Baker, John and Arlene Fox, and black leaders and writers of their generation—such as A. Philip Randolph, Bayard Rustin, Richard Wright, and Ralph Ellison—did not urge the importance of · color as much as they found color imposed on them in ways that affronted something inside them that was not black at all, or was black only ironically, or even absurdly, as Ellison would portray it. Proud though they were of what blacks had endured and overcome (as Baker "knew" they would), they shared with whites an important belief—not yet, alas, a consensus that racism was wrong, but a certainty that even despite it, they were all bound passionately to the promise of the nation.

Soon after the war in which Baker fought, that certainty became the country's best weapon against racism itself. If General Colin Powell succeeded Lieutenant Baker, it was thanks not only to affirmative action and other explicitly racial remedies but also to what people like Baker had affirmed and embodied: an America incandescent with a promise that cannot be comprehended by race. Neither blackness nor whiteness could be of much use in fulfilling that promise, for blackness was, at best, the noble survivor of a whiteness that had no coherent meaning outside of its oppression of blacks.

But what is that national promise? Whatever the answer, nothing can come of it if we fear letting go of race because we think that we would have nothing of value to say or give to one another once racism lost all weight in our social equations or disappeared entirely through interracial marriages and offspring. If we find it difficult now to say that a black person's color isn't important, it is because we no longer know how to say that being an "American" is important enough to transcend racial identity in a classroom, in a jury room, or at the polls.

As the writer James Alan McPherson posed the black American experience of this dilemma, in a 1993 essay, ·

> ... something very tragic happened to a large segment of the
> black American group during the past two decades. Whatever the

causes of this difficulty were, I believe that they were rooted more in the quality of our relation to the broader society than in defects in our own ethos. That is to say, we entered the broader society just at a time when there was the beginning of a transformation of its basic values. The causes of this transformation are a matter of speculation. In my own view, we became integrated into a special kind of decadence . . . one which leads to personal demoralization.

The problem is indeed deeper than racism. It is that, since the 1960s, whites have opened doors to admit blacks into a great civic and cultural hall whose walls have been falling down. As early as thirty-five years ago, writer James Baldwin asked, "Do I really *want* to be integrated into a burning house?" It's a good question, asked not about a brick-and-mortar structure but a spiritual and emotional home.

For hundreds of years, the very rigidity of racism in our triumphalist national procession gave blacks at least some moral footholds in their struggle to belong to the society into which they had been plunged, yet from which they were kept apart. But American blackness cannot sustain itself in "solidarity" against a whiteness that no longer knows itself, and no longer should. Black Americans who cling to fantasies of a separate racial destiny are doomed to careen in unanswered reproach and desperate flailing, from O. J. Simpson's acquittal to Ebonics, from Farrakhan's pseudo-Islamic gew-gaws and posturings of defiance to the bizarre "exoneration" of Martin Luther King, Jr.'s murderer, James Earl Ray, by King's own son Dexter and other members of his family who seem bent on uncovering a much wider conspiracy.

There will be no racial justice until blacks are willing to affirm—and whites, at last, are ready to understand—that the descendants of slaves are in some ways the most "American" of us all: Precisely because this is a society which blacks didn't choose to join and cannot hope to dominate, yet cannot really leave, they have much more at stake in society's fulfilling its stated, oft-violated promises than most of the rest of us comprehend. There always will and should be communities based on common memory, loss and longing and pride, but the best that blacks can expect of the rest of us (and the most that most have ever asked of us) is to embrace and judge them—and to let ourselves be embraced and judged by them—as individual participants in a common national experiment. As brothers, some used to say. Only a joint renunciation of blackness and whiteness as arbiters of our public life can lift the burdens of white supremacy and a retaliatory black demagoguery.

The black religious historian C. Eric Lincoln recalls that, since growing up under segregation during the 1920s, he has thought of white liberals as "friends who have done something to relieve me of the ponderousness of a system that is bearing down on me all the time." But many of today's liberals betray blacks by casting them all as the bearers of disadvantage and aggrievement whose end is not in sight. Like the old segregationist establishment, the new liberal racist one has black retainers including "critics" such as the law professor Derrick Bell, the black historian Robin D. G. Kelley, and the political minstrel and street-theater impresario the Reverend Al Sharpton, who reinforce its illusions. They abet liberal racism by telling professional antiracists what they want to hear, without expecting or effecting substantive change. Today's liberal racist establishment notoriously lacks the self-confidence and self-definition of its predecessors; what it wants, as I have noted, are ritual condemnations of its racism that implicitly credit its virtue.

Those who know how to deliver such condemnations profit handsomely. It is one thing to defend a community that has developed a distinct identity in oppression. It is another to foresee a Sisyphian struggle against racism that will never end. "Racism is an integral, permanent, and indestructible component of this society," writes Derrick Bell. The blackness he, Kelley, and Sharpton espouse is oppositional only, as if they were saying, "I am excluded; therefore, I am." Full inclusion would bring their implosion. So would full exclusion, of course; so they strike evasive, sometimes ingratiating poses of dignity-in-adversity, resisting inclusion just gently and sorrowfully enough to make white liberals uneasy and eager to offer support. Playing this game involves finding racism in every leaf that falls while relying on reservoirs of white racial guilt and deference whose existence black racists deny even as they accept media pulpits, book royalties, academic tenure, and constitutional protections.

Nice work, if you can get it—and skilled race pros certainly do. Robin Kelley's New York University voice-mail message, when I called in March 1997, included this advice:

> . . . If you're calling about speaking engagements, reading a manuscript, serving as a consultant, joining an editorial board, participating in a conference, or writing an essay, the answer is probably no: I will not be undertaking any new projects until the spring of 1998. Thank you very much.

At Harvard, the black leftist philosopher and preacher Cornel West's machine included the following:

> . . . At the beep, please leave a detailed message and it will be personally relayed to Professor West. Due to the high volume of calls, it is impossible for him to respond to all the calls received. Please understand that Professor West appreciates your interest, and we respectfully request that you do not call a second time. If you are calling concerning a Harvard engagement, please leave a message for [name, number]. For outside engagements, please call Professor West's agent [name and number in New York]. Thank you for calling.

Such are the wages of oppression. Even the old calypso Louis Farrakhan fascinates many white liberals, but since he goes too far, he gets overtures from conservatives like Jack Kemp and the columnist Robert Novak.

Our destiny hinges on whether countless individual blacks and whites can leave the old black-white embrace to create a new culture together, as we see and feel some doing every day. A lot depends on the steadiness and good sense of people who won't be corralled or stampeded in the name of race loyalty or racial guilt.

◆ Where To?

"Everybody has two heritages: ethnic and human," says the black jazz musician Wynton Marsalis. "The human aspects give art its real enduring power. . . . The racial aspect, that's a crutch so that you don't have to go out into the world. Jazz music teaches you what it is to live in a democracy, to be American." That is the astonishing story that unsung civic heroes, from Vernon Baker to Rafael Olmeda, are trying to tell and to live every day. Their Americanism is no more conservative than jazz or baseball. Its ethos is what the American literary historian Daniel Aaron calls "ethical and pragmatic, disciplined and free." It confounds the liberal imagination because it scrambles its moralistic and ideological thinking. That is why a rediscovery of American civic traditions can spare us the Balkanization and religious absolutism that grip so much of the rest of the world.

When it is well told and well lived, our civic story has two levels. On one, many Americans ground their personal dignity in ethnic and religious subcultures, the best of which prompt universal aspirations even while providing for their own members along parochial lines. On a second level, many of the same Americans "graduate" into a national civic culture, some of it drawn from their subcultures yet transcendent of them. When the larger civic culture is alluring enough, ethnic enclaves become staging grounds for transethnic leaders. The rural yet outward-facing Southern black Baptist subculture taught something about the promise of America not only to Martin Luther King, Jr., and his followers, but, through them, to many whites as well.

"The law can open doors and knock down walls, but it cannot build bridges," Thurgood Marshall wrote. "We will only attain freedom if we learn to appreciate what is different and muster the courage to discover what is fundamentally the same." Do we violate that vision and betray its raceless promise? All the time. Mid-century liberalism's greatest achievement was to assail and stop such violations more than ever before in our history. The new liberal racism is reviving them in sugarcoated but poisonous form.

Full citizenship in the American republic entails a commitment to join in a race-transcendent human experiment. Our civic culture cannot be blueprinted or parceled out along race lines. We affirm individual dignity when we refuse to treat any citizen as the delegate of a subculture or race. Our best leaders are those who show their neighbors, every day, how to leave subgroup loyalties at the doors of classrooms, jury rooms, hiring halls, and loan offices. They will embrace liberalism's preeminent challenge: to dissolve the color line by ceasing to treat whiteness and blackness as vessels of hope.

CHAPTER 2

INNOCENCE BY ASSOCIATION

◆ Color-coding Crime

Six days before Christmas 1996, Charles Davis, a New York City police officer, was slain with the owner of a check-cashing store where he was moonlighting to make extra money to buy holiday gifts for his six-year-old daughter, Arielle. By all accounts, Davis, thirty-eight, was an adoring father who put Arielle to bed every night, making her giggle with funny jigs and sweet songs. He and his wife, a former assistant district attorney, "were just two people who you could see were totally wrapped up in each other," a friend told the *New York Times*. By accounts that transcend the pieties one usually hears at funerals, Davis was a *very* good cop, and a tough one. He was popular not only with fellow officers but also with residents of the Queens neighborhood where he ran youth basketball tournaments and an organization for kids who might want to join the New York Police Department. His large presence, sharp eye, and obvious caring strengthened "community policing," which had helped cut the city's murder rate in half in less than five years. When he was killed on December 19, the 1996 rate hovered below one thousand for the first time in three decades.

Davis died while throwing his body in front of the check-cashing store's owner, Ira Epstein, forty, in a futile effort to protect him from being murdered, too. These two men, who contributed nothing to the city's glitter but much to its glue, were destroyed in a botched robbery attempt by two or three young black men. Apprehended by police, nineteen-year-old George Bell readily acknowledged that he had pulled the trigger. During a break in the questioning, he hummed, "Have Yourself a Very Merry Christmas," then got scared and kept asking what would happen to him. Remorse never seemed to enter his mind.

In keeping with Jewish custom, Epstein was buried quietly the day after his death. Officer Davis's Episcopal funeral mass a week later in suburban Garden City, Long Island, was a vivid "tableau of pomp and grief," as the *Times* put it, replete with thousands of saluting, white-gloved officers, a somber Mayor Rudolph Giuliani and Governor George Pataki, the police Emerald Society's mournful bagpiping, and a fly-over by police helicopters. "Arielle, your daddy, who loved you, who adored you, who cared for you, will always be a hero of New York City," Giuliani told Davis's daughter from the pulpit. The mayor asked the congregation to give Arielle something she would remember, and all present responded with a long, wrenching ovation. Giuliani noted that Ira Epstein's widow had told him that Davis was a role model for the city's youth. "She was right," he said, calling Davis "an example of what it means to be a real man. . . . When he died Saturday morning he was doing what he was trained to do—he was trying to protect another man."

If funerals such as Davis's are tableaux of pomp and grief, typically they are also dramatic renderings of the chasm between inner-city blacks and suburban ethnic whites, between the so-called "underclass" and the so-called "occupying army" of police in the ghetto. Not to put too fine a point on it, spectacles of slain officers, grieving families, and ranks of police in parade dress seldom fire the liberal civic imagination. (Certainly there was no outcry from liberal activists or institutions over Davis's murder.) Liberals who can recite with near reverence a roll call of black victims of white hatred—Rodney King,

Yusuf Hawkins (a black youth set upon and murdered by a gang of whites as he walked innocently through their Brooklyn neighborhood), Michael Griffith (chased by young whites to his death on a parkway in Queens's Howard Beach), Darrell Cabey (paralyzed for life by subway gunman Bernhard Goetz in 1984), and many others—would be hard put to recall whites murdered by blacks, especially if the victims are police officers.

But liberals forgot Charles Davis for a different, more troubling reason: He, like his killers, was black. That barred him from the pantheon of martyrs that would have received him had his killers been white. In a cruel irony, some of the black victims who did gain admission to that pantheon had records of criminal violence, like the men who killed Charles Davis. But this discrepancy in public attention is more than an irony; it is an indictment of liberal racism, which draws from the history of racism the false lesson that racial differences are far more profound than they really are—and, for some blacks, far more exculpatory than they really should be.

Just as murders register more strongly in the traditional racist imagination when committed by blacks against whites, they register more strongly in today's liberal imagination when committed by whites against blacks. Both mind-sets, blinded by color, eclipse the human reality that transcends it. In reality, most murders involve perpetrators and victims of the same race. In reality, proportionately more such murders are black-on-black than white-on-white. In reality, according to the Federal Bureau of Criminal Justice Services, more blacks in the United States are killed by other blacks in a single day than are killed by whites in a week. Yet black victim after black victim is lowered into urban America's choking soil without a word from any liberal commentator, activist, or politician, black or white.

Charles Davis was one of those victims. Once upon a time, he would have been a liberal hero in death, because he would already have been a liberal hero in life. He wasn't New York City's first heroic black cop, but his winning personality and his effectiveness with fellow officers and the public transcended race in ways liberals used to admire. Surely he did more to break down racism in the NYPD than any critic of police racism has done. Yet, now, he seemed as invisible to most liberals as he would have been vivid to their predecessors. When he was killed, there were no memorials to Davis or expressions of outrage toward the suspects by liberal advocacy groups whose members had taken to the streets over white-on-black murders. There were no protests by Al Sharpton, New York's premier impresario of racial street theater.

The wonder is that liberal racial moralists have been so slow to understand that racism is more likely to be diminished when transracial standards are strongly upheld. In a 1992 speech, "Race and the American City," former New Jersey senator Bill Bradley lamented that many whites, stunned by rising urban violence, wanted to say to some black males, "You litter the street and deface the subway, and no one, black or white, says stop. . . . You snatch a purse, you crash a concert, break a telephone box, and no one, white or black, says stop. You rob a store, rape a jogger, shoot a tourist, and when they catch you, if they catch you, you cry racism. And nobody, white or black, says stop."

Why? Now that the City of New York has, through its policing of minor "quality of life" offenses, posted a sign saying "Stop," many of its residents have discovered that not only is it not racist to do so, it enhances a sense of public order and helps to reduce the murder rate in poor, nonwhite neighborhoods more than anywhere else. That hasn't stopped people like Sharpton from crying that police brutality is rising—and it *shouldn't* stop him and others from protesting it, or a city from punishing it. But it should remind liberals that when society takes blacks seriously enough as individuals to condemn and punish them whenever they do wrong, it is more likely to provide all its citizens, but especially its black citizens, with safety and a sense of decency in public places.

◆ Turning the Tide

The renouncing of the inaction Bradley described didn't begin because liberals, both white and black, repented their tendency to exempt blacks from moral reproach. It began with a surge of feminist outrage, especially at black men's assaults on white women. It was high-profile trials involving such assaults that changed public reckonings about race, prompting people who weren't racists to speak up without fear of being misconstrued.

The rape and near murder of a white female jogger in Central Park in 1989 by young black and Hispanic men unleashed a torrent of white rage. That rage summoned the worst specters of black history, prompting the black *Amsterdam News* editor, Wilbert Tatum, and a number of activists to insist that the trial was "a lynching," reminiscent of a hundred years of hanging innocent black men accused of merely looking the wrong way at white women. However, few acquiesced in that kind of defense in this case; a black minister led a vigil for the victim, even as Sharpton brought Tawana Brawley—whose false charges of rape against white men in 1987 had already been exposed—to the jogger-trial courthouse to shake hands with the defendants, one of whom had already confessed while viewing photographs of the woman he had battered.

Brawley and Sharpton's tale had aroused and then betrayed widespread sympathy for her and outrage against white-male sexism and racism. In the jogger case, the tide turned: Women whose hearts had gone out to Brawley weren't about to let charges that the defendants were being "lynched" supersede charges of sexist abuse. Certainly they had no tolerance for lies like those told by the radical lawyer William Kunstler during the Brawley case: "It makes no difference whether the attack . . . really happened," he said as her tale unraveled. "The black community knows that there are a lot of Tawanas out there." But are there? Would Kunstler have considered it racist to note that, again according to federal statistics, for every black woman who is raped by a white man, at least five white women are raped by black men?

Few people believe that the long, sordid history of rapes of black women by whites excuses Kunstler's dissembling, which exemplified the leftist racism that robs blacks of personal dignity by turning them into mere props or character actors in antiracist theatrics. The one cruel irony in the otherwise salutary rejection of Kunstlerite thinking was that, the same week as the Central Park rape and beating, the rape and murder of a black woman by black men on a housingproject rooftop in Brooklyn attracted no more attention than Kunstler himself would have given it. Only when some news reports drew attention to that contrast did Donald Trump, who had taken out a full-page ad to express his outrage and demand justice in the jogger assault, send a donation to Brooklyn. A black observer might legitimately have felt that whites were simply turning their backs, not correcting the imbalances on both sides.

Then came the murders in Los Angeles in 1994 of Nicole Brown Simpson and Ronald Goldman, charged not to hapless youths but to a wealthy black celebrity whom many whites had admired, befriended, or loved. Now liberals had to choose clearly between, on the one hand, knee-jerk excuses for blacks who violate basic standards of decency and, on the other, tough affirmations of individual responsibility that transcend race. In the name of redressing racism, too many liberals dodge such choices every day by race-norming their decisions and trimming their candor in academic departments, classrooms, newsrooms, political meetings, and casual encounters. But now, in the same name of redressing racism, Johnnie Cochran transformed the trial of O. J. Simpson for murder into the trial of Los Angeles police officer Mark Fuhrman for his racist abuses of black people.

Not only were liberals appalled; some understood that Cochran, no less than Kunstler, was abusing black dignity by grasping for one standard of justice at the expense of another. Even as Cochran rightly condemned an abuse whose depth and power cannot be denied—that some police officers keep law-abiding blacks in a constant state of low-grade intimidation—he was manipulating that reality to distract attention from Simpson's, where it didn't apply or, even if it did, shouldn't have been decisive. Blacks deserve better ways to make whites acknowledge and curb racist abuses. The deliberate coloring of trials with racial histories and loyalties retards reform and separates the races even further. It reinforces racial resentments by turning individual victims, perpetrators, and even jurors into racial delegates, diminishing their dignity. If anything, Simpson's criminal acquittal based on Cochran's argument recalled the dark days when white juries often acquitted white killers of blacks such as NAACP leader Medgar Evers.

The civil rights movement rejected such tit-for-tat responses, even in the teeth of open racism. Its disciplined, loving tactics shamed whites by making calculated appeals to their integrity even while exposing their shortcomings. So doing, it sowed seeds that were still bearing fruit in the 1994 retrial and conviction of Evers's assassin. In contrast, Cochran's victory in a case that shouldn't have turned on race deepened black isolation. He made an important point at a price so steep that it has almost eclipsed the point he was trying to make.

◆ A New Reckoning?

What, really, *is* the best way to puncture white denial about racism? Liberals may describe fifty-seven varieties of white hostility, condescension, and myopia, but if their estimates of racism were more realistic, their risks and strategies against it would be shrewder, more supple, and more effective. Are those who want an honest conversation about police abuse willing to have ordinary police officers at the table? Are liberals willing to learn what decent cops see on patrol that prods or tempts some of them to act badly? In an essay in the December 12, 1990, issue of the socialist weekly *In These Times*, the writer Salim Muwakkil described his torments as a black man whose presence in Chicago's Loop after dark prompts sickeningly predictable responses from purse-clutching women and hostile cops. Then he added, as few others do, "But what about the indignities forced on those frightened by my approach? Their fear is a demanding burden. But it's a fear confirmed by crime statistics, if not experience. The police, to whom I fit a 'profile,' certainly are playing the odds when they stop me. . . . The tensions produced by these differing, though equally valid, perceptions are unravelling the civic culture."

What does it cost Muwakkil, and blacks generally, to make that admission? I think it costs far less than it does to deny the odds the police are playing. Are liberals, black or white, willing to be candid about what those odds reveal? It isn't enough to blame racism and strike "Fight the Power" poses on behalf of criminal defendants and demagogues. Such postures rely, ironically, on substantial reservoirs of white guilt, goodwill, and constitutional protection, even while denying the very existence of these goods. Fortunately, one can do that for only so long. After the Brawley hoax, the civil rights convictions of Rodney King's assailants, and the Simpson civil trial verdict, race hustlers such as Cochran, Sharpton, and their apologists may be finding it more difficult to sidetrack judgments of personal responsibility by charging racism. The more difficult that becomes, ironically, the easier it will be to win some ground against racism itself.

In the meantime, stripped of the exemptions from moral and intellectual standards which too many legal activists, journalists, university administrators, foundation officers, and activists granted them, impresarios of racial theater are floundering. After the Simpson criminal verdict, Cornel West, author of the bestselling book *Race Matters*, made a tortured argument, backed by no evidence, that the murders in Brentwood must have been committed not by O. J. Simpson but by some itinerant drug dealer, his race conveniently unknown. Similarly, years earlier, Kunstler (who died in 1995) told *American Lawyer* magazine that he had agonized about putting personal responsibility above race by defending Pang Ching Lam, a Chinese immigrant storeowner who had killed a black intruder. "It was the first time I had ever represented someone who killed a black person," Kunstler recalled. "Pang was Third World . . . it was clearly self-defense. And even then I had misgivings. . . . I'm not sure if Pang had been white that I would have taken [the case]." Had Pang been white, and had the black intruder killed him, Kunstler would probably have defended the intruder. Had Charles Davis been white,

Kunstler might well have defended those charged with his murder, more so because Davis had been a cop. That Davis was a *black* cop who died trying to protect a white man would have left even the mellifluous Kunstler tongue-tied.

Aside from Pang, Kunstler never did defend anyone, black or not, who was charged with harming a black person. The only time he ever came close was in 1981, when a young black man named Wayne Williams was charged in a horrifying string of murders of black boys in Atlanta. Kunstler descended upon the city in a media blaze with fellow lawyer Alan Dershowitz, proclaiming Williams the innocent fall guy for redneck conspirators who, the lawyers charged, were being hidden by the Georgia Bureau of Investigation. Good reporters and investigators, including Atlanta's black police chief Lee Brown, later the national drug czar, proved Kunstler and Dershowitz wrong.

In 1994, when Kunstler and his associate Ronald Kuby were trying to represent Colin Ferguson, a black man who gunned down passengers on a Long Island Rail Road train, I asked them whether they would want to do so had Ferguson been charged with murdering blacks, not whites. They admitted that they wouldn't; the point of their effort on Ferguson's behalf was to introduce the idea of a "black rage" defense. Joel Dreyfuss, a founder of the National Association of Black Journalists, called this an insult to blacks that reflects "white liberalism's tolerance of blacks based on a deficit model. . . . According to the 'black rage' defense, black folks are barely able to control themselves."

The Kunstlerite mind-set wouldn't matter very much were it a sectarian anomaly among liberal approaches to criminal justice. But it is a perfectly logical extension of many liberals' tendency to subordinate affirmations of personal responsibility and color-blind justice to claims that such standards are inherently racist. Even as most of the public rejects such thinking, we find it gaining ground now in important law schools and on many national stages besides the one where Cochran told Simpson's jurors to "send a message." The many lawyers, activists, and journalists who honor Kunstler's memory are among its bearers. A year after his death, a committee of the New York Civil Liberties Union's board of directors voted to hold an event in Kunstler's name; only a vigorous dissent by New York Civil Rights Coalition director Michael Meyers dissuaded his colleagues.

Liberal racists' indifference to every outrage they can't recast as a confrontation with white bigotry is an insult and a danger to every Charles Davis. It cedes the political initiative to conservative racists, except when law-and-order centrists like New York's Mayor Giuliani emerge to save liberals from themselves. How long it now seems since the time when liberals would have taken heart, even in tragedy, from the fact that the clergy and most of the congregation whom Giuliani addressed at Davis's funeral were black; that, still, the throng was racially well-integrated; and that most of the thousands of cops honoring Davis's memory and supporting his widow were white. Now there is only silence. In life, as in the circumstances of his death, Davis confounded too many liberal presumptions.

◆ Liberal Racism's Writ Runs Out

One thing that did tweak liberal sensibilities two years before Davis's death was Giuliani's aggressive policing of "quality of life" and other minor-crime infractions—the strategy that later yielded the suspects in Davis's case. "Quality of life" enforcement was begun under David Dinkins, the city's first black mayor, but when Giuliani, his successor, intensified it, it was denounced as the harbinger of a police state by lawyers for the Legal Aid Society, the executive director of the New York Civil Liberties Union, the usual assortment of left-liberal activists, and liberal editorial writers and columnists. Misdemeanor enforcement was little more than an excuse for police brutality, declared New York Supreme Court judge Bruce Wright, a liberal black jurist whom cops called "Turn 'Em Loose Bruce."

Yet George Bell and three other suspects in the murders of

Davis and Epstein were apprehended separately, as a citywide dragnet prompted by the murders brought in hundreds of people who had already been issued warrants for petty crimes. There are several reasons for issuing more desk warrants and summonses for petty offenses, and then following up on them in serious cases like these. First, policing minor, "quality of life" offenses—especially in poor neighborhoods where graffiti writing, littering, drinking on the street, and petty vandalism are routine—makes life more pleasant and dignified for the law-abiding residents. Second, as criminologist George Kelling has shown, restoring a sense of public order discourages criminal activity among people acutely aware of shifts in local conditions. Finally, and in the Davis/Epstein case most importantly, enforcing minor-crime laws generates names and addresses of people who have often committed more serious crimes—or are about to commit them, like subway fare-beaters who are found packing guns when they are arrested for leaping over turnstiles. After the murders of Davis and Epstein, it was Mark Bigweh, twenty, rounded up on charges of selling a five-dollar bag of marijuana, who acknowledged that he had been present when Davis and Epstein died and who then led cops to Bell.

The first and most important beneficiaries of Giuliani's "quality of life" policing—against panhandlers, drug addicts, and vandals in city parks and other public spaces—were poor black and Hispanic tenement dwellers, who, lacking yards, let alone vacation homes, need green oases and recreation facilities. Only as conditions in such places improved during the mid-1990s did self-styled advocates for the nonwhite poor begin to moderate their protests. Liberal advocates had also denounced as "racism" the aggressive apprehensions of young men caught jumping subway turnstiles, but a surprisingly high proportion of "fare-beaters" were found to be carrying weapons, and, with their arrests, crime in the subways dropped dramatically. Only then, it seemed, did those who had characterized the fare-beaters as victims of racism notice how many law-abiding black and Hispanic people depended on safe subways.

It seems, however, that racial poseurs cannot learn from substantive gains. Two weeks after Giuliani's inauguration in 1994, producers of the racial demonstrations that had convulsed the city in the Howard Beach, Tawana Brawley, Bensonhurst, Central Park Jogger, Crown Heights, and other bloody cases stood with the Reverend Al Sharpton as he declared that cops' attempt to enter a Nation of Islam mosque in Harlem to answer a robbery call was "the opening round of [Giuliani's] war on black New Yorkers." (Actually, the only people injured were cops, one of them female, whom worshippers had shoved down the stairs as the officers tried to enter the mosque.) Nearly a year later, Sharpton led two hundred marchers to disrupt Christmas shopping on Fifth Avenue in a protest against what he insisted was an unprecedented surge in police brutality since Giuliani had taken over from David Dinkins, the city's first black mayor. But, in the eleven months between the mosque incident and the march, the city's homicide rate had dropped 18 percent, which meant that perhaps two hundred African Americans who would otherwise have been murdered were still walking around. Even had Giuliani deserved no credit for the gains in public safety, it was hard to see how he deserved condemnation. When I mentioned this to Sharpton during a television debate, he blinked; that all those lives had been saved seemed not to have occurred to him. What had really bothered black politicians and liberal media commentators about the mosque incident was that Giuliani, who considered it a police matter and not an occasion for high-level diplomacy, had refused to meet with Sharpton and others claiming to represent "the black community" in the matter.

Had Giuliani been playing racial politics, he might have capitalized on the incident to claim that black nationalists are violent and antipolice. He refused to do that, too. "I don't have a special message for any group," he said. "People in this city don't need special things. They need more of certain general things—safety, education, jobs. The officers who went into that mosque didn't ask the color or gender of the people they were trying to protect. That's how most

New Yorkers conduct themselves, and it's how I'll run this administration."

After the tortuous racial etiquette of liberals' "gorgeous mosaic" politics, such professions of race neutrality sound almost otherworldly. Liberals suspect that such talk masks racial double standards. Giuliani hasn't always resisted temptations to play ethnic and racial politics, but he neither baits nor condescends to racial provocateurs, and his comments about the mosque incident were consistent with his message almost three years later, by which time Harlem's homicide rate had dropped 67 percent: He hadn't done anything for black New Yorkers, he said, but for the whole city.

But the politics of racial posturing dies hard. When a dead tree in a middle-class black neighborhood fell on a van, crushing four black children to death, Sharpton charged that Giuliani had failed to prune the trees in black neighborhoods—until it emerged that it was Dinkins who had decimated the city's tree pruners in an austerity move and that Giuliani had restored some. In another dispute, two black city council members denounced Giuliani's observation that safety is the most important "civil right"—until they learned that Dinkins had said it first. In Brooklyn, a police officer killed a black minister's son, drawing Sharpton to the scene, cameras in tow—until he learned that the officer, too, was black and had shot the young man, a drug dealer, in a raid on a drug den. During Giuliani's first three months in office, two blacks were killed by black police officers, and two white cops were killed by nonwhites. No one drew racial conclusions from this body count, because there were none to be drawn.

The eradication of criminal violence should be a primary goal of any society and, indeed, of any social movement. Only someone possessed by racialist fantasies can conceive of criminal violence as a force for justice. Even Karl Marx, who cautioned his followers against romanticizing the victims of capitalist oppression, would have dismissed advocates like William Kunstler with contempt.

◆ Liberal Rationalizations

But what about the "root causes" of criminal violence? Consider a response that exemplifies white liberal denial not of racism but of racial equality. In 1992, the Los Angeles riots made a bestseller of white political scientist Andrew Hacker's *Two Nations: Separate, Hostile, and Unequal*, which attempted to convict whites of being more deeply racist than they think they are. In Hacker's view, if more blacks are killed by other blacks every day than are killed by whites in a week, this is because racism is more insidiously demoralizing now than when it was formally institutionalized. According to Hacker, "While in one sense these [killings of blacks by other blacks] are 'free acts,' . . . they must also be seen as expressing a despair that suffuses much of their race. . . . It is white America that has made being black so disconsolate an estate." The root of the problem, Hacker thinks, is not only that many cops are bigots but that they act on behalf of a white consensus about blacks that becomes a self-fulfilling prophecy as blacks internalize it from childhood on. Unlike avowed segregationists, Hacker warns, most whites have managed to isolate and condemn blacks without spelling out what they're doing. In Hacker's view, white contempt not only makes it easy to blame the victim, it makes the victims blame themselves.

There is truth here, but it is not the whole truth, and we are well past the time when anything can be gained by denying blacks a larger measure of both credit and responsibility for their own liberation, even in the teeth of racism itself. Hacker cannot imagine such a liberation. Giuliani is sustained by "a fear [white] vote," he said on a New York 1 News television program late in 1993, characterizing the candidate as the political creation of whites who think, "It used to be our city and 'they' are taking it away. . . ." Again, racial symbolism eclipsed reality: Giuliani won 38 percent of the Hispanic vote and 77 percent of the Asian vote. (He won only 5 percent of the black vote because he was running against the city's first black mayor and was being characterized by Dinkins supporters as a "fascist" and "racist" and by the *New York Times* as an apostle of "civic Reaganism" and a champion of white-ethnic restoration.) "Crime, welfare, drugs, guns—all those have a black coloration" in the election, Hacker insisted, surely thinking that he was speaking only of whites who "want a certain kind of city; they want the troublemakers controlled. . . ."

"Don't *you?*" interrupted Peter Medona, a gentle Bronx baker also on the television program who had been one of the "Faces of Hope" at Bill Clinton's 1993 inauguration. Hacker sputtered, spread his hands, and said not a word. Medona had caught him applying to all whites the insidious "they" which bigoted whites apply so roundly to blacks. Hacker's disdain for working-class white ethnics is unrelenting and palpably aristocratic. But there is also a hint of racial self-loathing. Lynne Duke, a black reporter for the *Washington Post*, asked Hacker whether he thinks himself exempt from the evils he attributes to whites. "Oh, believe me," he replied, "I need my whiteness as much as Joe the truck driver does." Or Pete the baker?

And there is even a hint of displaced racism, a contempt for blacks, which seeps out of Hacker's own prose even as he struggles to project it onto working-class whites. Reviewing *Two Nations*, the black economist and social critic Glenn Loury called the book an example of "liberal racism" that portrays black Americans "as a confused, defeated, and disturbed collection of people, obsessed with what whites have done to them and incapable of doing anything for themselves. . . ." Loury condemned "Hacker's refusal to take blacks seriously, as morally responsible agents capable of shaping their lives according to their will. . . ."

Similar concerns were raised even in the liberal *New York Review of Books*, to which Hacker frequently contributes, by David Brion Davis, the distinguished (white) historian of slavery, who reviewed *Two Nations* in its July 16, 1992 issue. Hacker's assertions that blacks can't be expected to conform to "white" behavioral and intellectual standards because their racial culture is so distinctive "remind one of the romantic racialism of the past," Davis wrote, regretting that "Hacker is still partially trapped by the tendency . . . to make racial differences displace all other explanations of behavior. . . ."

But suppose that Hacker is right and that racism has forced blacks to internalize a despair so deep that their norms and values are different from ours. Surely a despair this profound cannot be dissolved by white repentance and reparations. That is why even blacks who wince at candor like Salim Muwakkil's also wince at Hacker's and other white liberals' moralistic contortions about racism. In Hacker's discussion of crime, the contortions become insulting. He observes, accurately, that violent crime is disproportionately black and that "black Americans have a three times greater chance than whites of dying from a policeman's bullet. As it happens," he continues, "a disproportionately high number of these killings of blacks are by black policemen, which suggests that departments tend to give black officers assignments where they encounter suspects of their own race. . . . There is a tendency to use blacks to control blacks." Here, analysis has given way to ideologically driven evasion. If proportionately more blacks than whites are dying from policemen's bullets, isn't that largely because—as Hacker's own findings affirm—violent crime is so heavily black? Isn't this all the more plausible if, as Hacker also reports, so many cops who kill blacks are themselves black? And what on earth is Hacker saying about departments' hiring policies? That they *shouldn't* hire more blacks? That they should assign fewer of them to black neighborhoods?

White cops often do misread cues in black youths' behavior. But if black cops are less likely to misread, they aren't necessarily more merciful. Perhaps, Hacker muses, "experience has jaundiced so many officers that they see even law-abiding blacks as belonging to the 'other side.' Compounding these stereotypes is the fact that the typical police officer is a high school graduate, from a working-class background, who had never previously set foot in the areas he now patrols. . . . And at least a few police officers still move in circles where no censure attaches to using the word 'nigger.' "

How does this explain why so many blacks are killed by black cops? It doesn't, of course. Hacker seems simply to have forgotten that there are black cops at all, and he's back to talking about "working class" whites who say "nigger." A discussion so skewed by denial of the glaring realities it has documented can't parse the real problem of police racism in a way that serves blacks or whites well. Hacker wants to show whites how hypocritical and indifferent they remain about the intolerable burden of being black in America. But when he mischaracterizes that burden and caricatures its sources by suggesting that police exams using words such as "disposition" and "unsubstantiated" are racially unfair, he only increases the burden of blackness and insults both races. His discussion of policing is an example of how racialist analysis slides from reality into cant. It's a mystery how liberals can posit a monolithic white world and a hapless black one—and at the same time hope to change either.

Like Hacker, the white writer Benjamin DeMott thinks that while irresponsible acts are in one sense "free," they're all but predestined by castelike poverty. Midway through his often-insightful *The Trouble with Friendship: Why Americans Can't Think Straight About Race*, DeMott laments the trial of Joyce Ann Moore, a black welfare mother in Milwaukee who was convicted in 1990 of homicidal neglect of six of her seven children after they burned to death when she left them alone at home one night. It wasn't the first time she'd left them unattended or permitted them to live amid such dangers as a kitchen floor smeared with feces. After a four-day trial, Moore was convicted and sentenced to seven years in prison.

The severity of the sentence is heartbreaking; Moore is unlikely to be a danger to other people's children. But DeMott is even more troubled by the conviction than by the sentence, and here, I think, he gets carried away in making what amounts to a liberal racist argument: Since society bears "responsibility for Moore's situation as a mother," he argues, the court's color-blind assumptions about personal responsibility should be mooted by her "bottom-caste" status as a school dropout, pregnant at fourteen, deserted by the three men whose children she bore, and lacking a family support system or public day care. "Black America includes millions of welfare mothers, the majority overwhelmed by their lives," DeMott declares. "But her case, like numberless parallel cases, is in-

structive . . . because of counsels' insistence on her capability.
Judicial denials of caste truth invariably begin with tacit agree-
ment, by the prosecution and the defense, that bottom-caste
defendants should be presented as free agents acting and exe-
cuting on their own. . . ."

Few black welfare mothers are as dysfunctional as Moore,
but to suspend judgment of her in deference to "caste" is
to desert and insult them all. Perhaps DeMott thinks they
shouldn't serve on juries or vote. Precisely because the imposition of caste is indeed an affront to personal dignity, liberal
justice should not reinforce it by erasing presumptions of personal capability. DeMott ought to check this with Nelson Mandela, or, for that matter, Farrakhan: Only by insisting on
personal responsibility can a movement against injustice uplift
and mobilize the oppressed.

"Much of the injury to African Americans caused by educational deprivation, demeaning job ceilings, and ascribed inferiority can be read in . . . street drunkenness, gang gunfire in
projects, whole schools engaged in teaching child-mothers
how to discharge parental responsibilities," DeMott reports,
adding, like Hacker, that the deepest damage is internalized in
self-defeat and self-loathing. Again, there is truth here, but
caste distinctions are reinforced, not eroded, by liberals who
equate moral censure with repression.

The "blame racism, not the victim" argument now has an
almost archaic sound. The tightening of many white liberals'
jaws in response to the Brawley hoax, the jogger-trial defense
strategies, and the Simpson verdict may signal the turning
tide, but, as we will see in Chapters 5 and 6, many blacks, too,
are rethinking the balance between personal and social
responsibility—with harsh consequences, incidentally, for
conservative as well as liberal doctrines that emphasize one
side or the other. Liberals must admit that their charges of
"racism" are often so extenuated and exotic that they reinforce racism by making blacks seem an exotic appendage to
the polity.

Since most liberals have qualms about saying this, they
grasp at other explanations: "Blame the economy as well as

racism; blame class as well as race." But, like DeMott's confla-
tion of race and caste to absolve Joyce Ann Moore of all moral
and legal responsibility in the deaths of her children, these
explanations don't tell the whole truth either. The most
important recent attempt to blame crime on a mix of class and
race is black sociologist William Julius Wilson's *When Work
Disappears*, a formidably detailed, very useful study of inner-
city Chicago that was grasped like a lifesaver by liberals whose
"racism" explanations were drowning empirically, politically,
and culturally.

As do Hacker and DeMott, Wilson portrays criminal behavior as a product of "factors beyond the control" of inner-
city residents. Like Hacker, Wilson provides evidence of
self-destructive behavior from which he doesn't draw cultural
and moral conclusions. He finds, for example, that many black
as well as white employers disdain young African-American
males but hire equally poor first-generation black and Hispanic immigrants, whose cultural habits and predispositions
make them reliable workers. Yet Wilson doesn't conclude that
findings like this weaken racial and economic excuses for
black unemployment and crime. Similarly, he laments that
jobs have gone to suburbia, "a particular problem for inner-
city blacks because they have less access to private auto-
mobiles and, unlike Mexicans, do not have a network system
that supports organized carpools." Yet he doesn't ask why
blacks don't set up carpools, too. Why such avoidance?

Larry Nachman, a professor at the College of Staten Island,
has an answer worth considering. Writing about Hacker's *Two
Nations*, Nachman characterizes the book's fundamental assumption this way: "If there are disparities . . . between blacks
and other Americans, it must be either because blacks are bio-
logically inferior or because of the . . . racist environment."
Since liberals who think this way rightly reject the false assumption of inferiority, they are left with only racism to
blame. But Nachman denies that racism renders blacks morally helpless. He marvels that Hacker doesn't recognize a third
possibility that presents blacks neither as inferior nor as hapless victims: "He cannot bring himself to think about elements
in black culture which might work against success."

To which one must add "elements in American culture," or, more precisely, liberal racists' cluelessness about how civic culture holds even poor societies together—including much more of black inner-city society than liberals themselves are prone to admit. Such myopia condemns liberals to continuing political defeat. Like Charles Davis, who grew up in low-income public housing in Brooklyn, many decent, hardworking blacks live near Joyce Ann Moore and her children without succumbing to despair. If the rest of the country is to encourage, instruct, and employ such people, liberal scholars, journalists, activists, and advocates must contribute something to a shared American moral consciousness besides hand-wringing and reproach.

Racism against black defendants in the criminal justice system is a great, historic wrong. Liberal activists, opinion makers, legislators, lawyers, and judges did much to curb it in the 1950s and '60s, and an unsung few continue to do so today. But lately liberals have been curbing systemic racism in favor of a racism that refuses to pay blacks the compliment of holding them to the same elementary civil standards as everyone else. Reforms based on rationalizations like Hacker's and DeMott's would only deepen the misery of black crime victims, at mounting cost to poor black neighborhoods' safety and morale. With stunning callousness, "civil rights" attorneys from Kunstler to Cochran have goaded black juries into political, "send a message" acquittals of black assailants of whites, never considering that not only are such acquittals morally indistinguishable from those of white assailants of blacks in the old South, they also encourage liberals' shameful neglect of black victims killed or raped by blacks.

The liberal racist diversion of crime fighting to shadow-boxing with "root causes" has been a tragic failure. It has so weakened public safety that it has undermined "progressive" political organizing, logistically and morally. The question isn't *whether* liberals have done this; it is *why they can't see that they have*—and why, instead of admitting that the tactics of Kunstler and Cochran and the rationalizations of Hacker and DeMott have backfired, they keep denouncing only white-on-black murderers, crime fighters such as Giuliani, church burners, and phantoms in black robes, blue suits, or white sheets. Finger-pointing at racist bogeymen, real and imagined, may bring liberals prompt, temporary relief from feelings of moral vacuity, but it doesn't advance justice. Instead of invigorating our public life and strengthening our faith in one another, it denies people like Charles Davis and his many emulators and mourners the nurture and the honor we owe them.

CHAPTER 3

VOTING WRONGS

◆ Losing Faith

"It is wrong—deadly wrong—to deny any of your fellow Americans the right to vote," Lyndon Johnson told a joint session of Congress on March 15, 1965, following a week of interracial marches led by blacks whom Sheriff Jim Clark had barred from registering at the courthouse of the old Alabama plantation town of Selma. Invoking the nation's "outraged conscience" after Clark's deputies and state troopers assaulted the marchers—among them a quiet, intense seminary student named John Lewis—Johnson said that it was time to overcome a "crippling legacy of bigotry and injustice." Then the president paused, looked up from his text at Congress and seventy million television viewers, and said—evenly, firmly, in his West Texas accent—"And we *shall* overcome."

Amid the long congressional ovation, some of the segregationists in Johnson's audience, such as Senator Strom Thurmond from South Carolina, sat stone-faced, their hands unmoving. "Watching the speech from Jean and Sullivan Jackson's living room in Selma, Martin King was overcome by emotion," writes David J. Garrow in his book *Bearing the Cross*. "His colleagues and friends had never seen him cry before. 'Tears actually came to Dr. King's eyes when President

Johnson said, "We shall overcome," ' John Lewis remembered. Never before, in nine years' time, had the movement received the breadth of national support, and the strength of federal endorsement, that this week had witnessed."

No one knew better than King that blacks could not hope to exercise the rights guaranteed them by the Fifteenth Amendment without the help of new laws, court rulings, administrative regulations, and enforcement by federal marshals and troops. Yet King knew, too, that something essential to blacks' vindication couldn't be legislated, mapped, or enforced: the strangely vulnerable faith he and millions of Americans shared with Johnson. If one believes that power belongs ultimately to ordinary people who are free to choose leaders and policies in the uncoerced privacy of voting booths, then one's only reliable support for that belief is what the historian Fred Siegel calls "the politics of persuasion," which instructs and moves people through cogent arguments and moral witness instead of manipulating or ordering them around. A politics of persuasion alone can't win justice, but, without it, freedom cannot exist.

In Siegel's view, liberals have stopped talking to the American people and fled to the courts and, I would add, to a moralistic journalism that censures "bad" thinking rather than persuades. Thirty years after Johnson had spoken, Newt Gingrich stood at the same podium, delivering his "inaugural" address as Speaker of a new Republican-run House of Representatives, and he surprised many by drawing his colleagues into an ovation to liberal Democrats and the civil rights movement: "No Republican here should kid themselves about it; the greatest leaders in fighting for an integrated America in the twentieth century were in the Democratic Party. The fact is, it was the liberal wing of the Democratic Party that ended segregation. . . . And the fact is, every Republican has much to learn from studying what the Democrats did right."

This time, it was liberal Democrats like Kweisi Mfume of Maryland and Nydia Velazquez of New York who sat stone-faced, their hands unmoving, looking for all the world as if they thought Gingrich's tribute a subtle ploy to divide his national audience by reminding whites whom to blame for color-coding politics. His subtext: "Thanks to you liberals, we can now transcend you and carry on your work at a higher level." For Gingrich, that "higher level" consisted not of more civil rights legislation, rulings, and enforcement, but of freer markets, which he believed would sweep away cobwebs of color and caste and stimulate the enlightened self-interest that sustains free communities and free selves.

The Speaker's unspoken point was that because liberals didn't understand this, they were compounding racial divisions they meant to heal and thickening cobwebs of suspicion they meant to dispel. "He's really tweaking liberals for being less committed to integration than *he* is," said a conservative acquaintance of mine, watching the speech. "What he really means is that Republicans should study what liberal Democrats did *wrong.*"

How had it come to this? Gingrich was at that podium in no small part because liberals had led in amending Johnson's original Voting Rights Act to intensify racial congressional districting, laying the groundwork for their own isolation and defeat. In order to produce more black and Hispanic Democrats like Mfume and Velazquez, the new districting plans packed minorities more tightly into "their own" districts. But doing this had the effect of whitening the neighboring districts, depriving incumbent white Democrats of reliably Democratic nonwhite voters and strengthening Republican challengers, enough of whom won to help the GOP take over the House. Liberals who seemed programmed to view these Republican victories as racist couldn't acknowledge, much less interpret, the fact that, after thirty years of liberal-led struggles to "overcome," the only two black members of the House that Gingrich was addressing who represented majority-*white* districts were *Republicans*—J. C. Watts of Oklahoma and Gary Franks of Connecticut. No liberal commentator, activist, advocate, or politician took note of this anomaly.

The story of how liberals blundered on voting rights is a wonderfully instructive parable of their noble beginnings and subsequent bad faith on many fronts touching race. It shows how racialist thinking, ethnocentrism, leftist ideology, moralism, and rank political opportunism have too often ganged up on the politics of persuasion, producing bad public policy and stifling the freedoms they claim to advance. Equally instructive is the story of liberal denial about the damage racial districting has done.

◆ From Empowerment to Apathy

After 1965, liberals made many precedent-setting revisions to voting rights legislation and jurisprudence, each well-intentioned, even imperative in its time. But the racial battle lines that evolved wouldn't have become so entrenched had liberals been smarter practitioners of the politics of persuasion. As voting rights activists tested the outer limits of liberal racism, they revealed a shocking misunderstanding of liberal democracy.

At first, the 1965 Voting Rights Act (VRA) made even segregationists like Strom Thurmond more responsive to blacks. Although he refused to applaud Johnson's speech, Thurmond began hiring black congressional staff as black enfranchisement grew, and he serviced his black constituents assiduously enough to win their support at the polls. The VRA also helped to increase the number of black elected officials nationwide, from fewer than 100 in 1965 to more than 2,500 today, by some counts. Most of them were chosen by heavily black electorates in local contests for lower offices. But the VRA helped to change white voters' attitudes, too: In 1966, Massachusetts's electorate, 80 percent white, made Edward Brooke the first black U.S. senator since Reconstruction. Herman Badillo won the Bronx borough presidency in New York City, also in 1966, when only 10 percent of Bronx voters were Hispanic. In 1972, Andrew Young was elected to Congress by a mostly white district in Atlanta. On similar terms, millions of white voters have since made L. Douglas Wilder the governor of Virginia, seat of the old Confederacy; Carol Moseley-Braun a senator from Illinois; a dozen blacks statewide officials in nearly as many states; another dozen the mayors of majority-white cities; and yet another dozen members of Congress from majority-white districts.

Still more to its credit, the original VRA curbed discriminatory racial districting. In such actions, politicians who belong to the party in power in a state often "gerrymander" its district lines into convoluted shapes to increase their partisan strength, packing loyal constituent groups into certain districts and removing them from others. Race has no appropriate relation to such partisan line-drawing, for individuals can change their interests, views, and political loyalties without changing the colors of their skins. For example, in the 1930s, blacks made a mass exodus from the party of Lincoln to the party of Franklin Roosevelt. But, back then, even in "liberal" states such as New York, blacks' conversion from Republican to Democrat didn't necessarily endear them to white Democrats, who tried to co-opt their votes with fine phrases and patronage crumbs, but kept shifting them around among districts to keep them from electing black Democrats.

Quite properly, the Voting Rights Act disrupted such hypocrisy. Enforced through bold, arduous litigation, it stopped district-line drawers from dispersing bits of otherwise coherent minority communities among mostly white districts in order to deny blacks homegrown representation. Thanks to a 1967 suit, for example, a long-standing concentration of black neighborhoods in Brooklyn, New York, whose potential clout had been parceled out among several mostly white congressional districts, was consolidated into one district that sent Shirley Chisholm to Congress the next year. The VRA made the bosses acknowledge that, whether through *de facto* segregation or voluntary affinity, a large black community did exist; that it encompassed several school districts, police precincts, and other jurisdictions; and that, like any other geographical community of whatever color (or mix of colors), it had a right to send one of its members to Congress. VRA suits also stopped bosses from changing the mechanisms for electing county commissioners and city councilmembers from district-based to at-large elections, which, in majority-white jurisdictions, kept minority-black voters from electing anyone of their own race.

But here we approach the line that liberals unwisely crossed. Despite dramatic black electoral gains under the Voting Rights Act, many activists, advocates, and journalists decided that whites' perceptions and interests would remain so irreconcilable with nonwhites' that few whites would ever vote for blacks or Hispanics. Therefore, they insisted, nonwhites' right to vote could be exercised meaningfully only if they were "empowered" to vote *en bloc,* as members of "protected" racial classes, in districts drawn to elect blacks or Hispanics. "That's an incredible expansion of the meaning of the right to vote," notes Abigail Thernstrom, author of *Whose Votes Count? Affirmative Action and Minority Voting Rights.* It was also an incredibly blind move toward what David Garrow calls "the unspoken assumption that black empowerment is a zero-sum game" against whites and that "justice means proportional representation by race."

None of this was envisioned in the original VRA. While it insisted that line drawers respect existing communities enough not to disperse their votes, it never confused defending the right to vote with presuming that blacks and Hispanics had an inherent need, and therefore a special "right," to elect candidates from racial groups to which all of them were presumed to belong politically. In states with long histories of segregation, blacks might indeed share many interests regardless of where and how they lived, and regardless of whether legal segregation had been abolished a few decades earlier. Yet some states' black populations were spread too thinly to form geographical communities. Worse yet for proponents of such racial communities, in 1980 the Supreme Court raised the standards of proof that district-line drawers who didn't create "black" or "Hispanic" districts were discriminating racially, not just gerrymandering for traditional, partisan reasons.

So, in 1982, liberal voting-rights activists and legislators amended the VRA to expand remedial racial districting. The motive was noble but the method mistaken: Instead of requiring proof that line drawers had intentionally discriminated, the new criteria measured a districting plan's fairness by comparing the proportion of a state's elected nonwhites to the proportion of its nonwhite residents. And instead of merely thwarting the backroom racial gerrymandering that had denied a community like black central Brooklyn the chance to send one of its own leaders to Congress, the amended VRA in effect told states whose numbers of black and Hispanic officials weren't proportionate to their black and Hispanic populations that they must actually create convoluted districts to produce officials of the right colors. Instead of just preventing racial gerrymandering, the new VRA, as interpreted by courts and enforced by the Justice Department, virtually ordered more of it for "protected classes," no matter how far apart from one another they lived and no matter how different their circumstances.

To satisfy this notion of "empowerment" by skin color or surname, the new districts resembled wild ink spills. In most states, Democratic-controlled legislatures did the redistricting, often making the new majority-minority districts even more convoluted than they had to be to satisfy the VRA; their partisan purpose was to keep *some* blacks and Hispanics in neighboring white Democrats' districts and give them an edge against Republican-leaning whites. The most telling objection to the new, tentacled districts wasn't that they were aesthetically displeasing; it was that they violated every notion of community except a racialist one.

New York City's new "Hispanic" congressional district, for example, created during the 1992 reapportionment, jumps from lower Manhattan across the East River to Brooklyn, and then runs overland for miles along corridors only a few blocks wide into Queens—all to connect dissimilar Hispanic enclaves. Dubbed "the Bullwinkle district" because of its shape, the 12th Congressional District's boundaries separate mothers on welfare in heavily Puerto Rican high-rise public housing projects on Manhattan's Lower East Side from mothers on welfare in similar but blacker projects nearby, in order to link the Puerto Ricans to working-class Mexican and Dominican immigrants in Brooklyn and to South American immigrant

homeowners in leafy neighborhoods in Queens. The district
slices through moderately integrated neighborhoods to create
an empty ethnic solidarity for people who have neither demanded it nor mobilized for it.

In the late 1970s, I ran a newspaper in Brooklyn's Williamsburg section, a gritty, polyglot area of Polish and Italian Americans, Orthodox Jewish Hasidim, and Dominicans and Puerto
Ricans. The 12th District's boundaries now slice through that
area to embrace only the Hispanic enclaves. At meetings of
the community planning boards and hospital advisory groups
where federal programs, services, and regulations are addressed, the Hispanics in the room now have one member of
Congress, many of the whites another. Even as such districting intensifies racial discord, a majority-minority district
created this way ensures its own voters' apathy by taking in
portions of so many different school districts, police precincts, and local election districts that its representative in
Congress cannot respond to them well.

This is not "empowerment"; it is an evisceration of civil
society and local democracy in the service of an ideology that
only a racist could endorse. So thought a plaintiff against the
12th District, Angel Diaz, who handles patient accounts at a
hospital in the area. Diaz didn't feel empowered at all by the
new district—and not just because he was the Republican
who had run against Velazquez in 1992. "It's irresponsible to
the American way of life to tell me I must agree with [the district's defenders] because I'm Puerto Rican," he told me. "By
cutting up my neighborhood, they left out some buildings
where I lived for twenty-seven years. So my friends there—a
few are Italian Americans—couldn't vote for me." The suggestion, aired in a *New York Times* news story, that Diaz might
lack standing to sue because he was Hispanic reflected racial
groupthink at its worst—unless one compared it to what a
Times editorial said on December 24, 1994, when majority-
black districts in North Carolina were invalidated after challenges by *white* resident plaintiffs: "There is no shortage of
people who want to block minority districts; their perverse
argument is that whites are the real victims of racial redistricting, and some courts are buying it."

The *Times* missed the point: While the law does constrain a plaintiff to show that he or she has been harmed, it is civic virtue, not racial self-interest, that makes suits against these districts legitimate. Ironically, and even more perversely, when white·Hasidim sued to abolish another majority-Hispanic district in Williamsburg in 1975, a more liberal Supreme Court found that, as whites, they had no standing because white members of Congress from districts nearby would represent them, even though the plaintiffs couldn't vote for them.

In 1992, the newly drawn 12th District elected Nydia Velazquez, whom we saw earlier refusing to applaud Gingrich's "inaugural" address two years later. A native of Puerto Rico, she had worked for five years as its government's liaison to Puerto Ricans in the United States, winning recognition in what would become the 12th District by running an Hispanic voter registration campaign financed by the Commonwealth of Puerto Rico. Velazquez spent so much time in such work that, in 1992, she spoke English poorly and seldom appeared on English-language programs. She has been reelected twice since then, but with the lowest voter turnout of any congressional district in the United States.

There is a double irony here: Under the VRA, the Justice Department had found two reasons to assume jurisdiction over the area in which the 12th District was later created. Ballots were not being provided in Spanish, and voter turnouts were low, supposedly reflecting line drawers' failure to empower Hispanics. But when Spanish-language ballots were readily available, and when the 12th was created under what a federal court would later call "misguided and unlawful instructions of the Department of Justice" that segregated Hispanics like Diaz from their immediate, non-Hispanic neighbors, turnout plummeted even further. In 1996, approximately 64,000 people voted in Velazquez's race, giving her 84 percent of the vote. Next door, in a redrawn version of the old Chisholm district, whose long-standing black community was represented by Major Owens, almost 90,000 people voted, even though Owens's assurance of reelection was even greater than Velazquez's. To the south, in a whiter district represented by Charles Schumer, the turnout was 129,000. Nationwide, the average congressional district turnout in that election was nearly 200,000. The Puerto Rican Legal Defense and Education Fund claims that low turnouts in the district reflect the high proportion of noncitizens, non-English-speakers, poor single mothers, and children under voting age. A more telling reason for the apathy is that liberals have created a Puerto Rican pacification program, replete with segregated voting, bilingual education that ghettoizes the young, and a district with so many geographical twists and turns that no local challenger to Velazquez could build support in enough of its far-flung communities to mount a serious campaign. It is as if liberals issued every Hispanic voter a pair of crutches to get to the polls, and then were surprised to see few turn up. The district is what the British would call a "rotten borough," in which elections are merely ceremonial. The fact is, in all such specially drawn "majority-minority" districts around the country, voter turnouts are fabulously low.

◆ Victory and Denial

Soon after the creation of districts like Velazquez's, the Supreme Court began ruling against making race the dominant factor in districting. Decisions invalidating some of the districts drove the race industry to howls of outrage and prophecies of doom: *Miller v. Johnson*, which knocked down two majority-black districts in Georgia in 1995, was "a definite setback," said Deval Patrick, Assistant U.S. Attorney General for Civil Rights. It portended "a return to the days of all-white government," warned ACLU voting rights specialist Laughlin McDonald. "The noose is tightening," said Elaine Jones, director-counsel of the NAACP Legal Defense and Education Fund; because of the rulings, said Theodore Shaw, the fund's associate director, the black congressional delegation would be able to fit "in the back of a taxicab." When the Court invalidated two Texas districts in *Bush v. Vera* in June 1996, Jesse Jackson foresaw "a kind of ethnic cleansing."

On November 5, 1996, five black incumbent members of

Congress whose black-majority districts had been eliminated by court orders faced the voters in new, nonblack-majority districts in Georgia, Florida, and Texas. And they all won, exploding the liberal certainty that whites so seldom vote for blacks that the latter can exercise their voting rights fully enough to elect a candidate of their choice (presumed to be of the same color) only when they're "empowered" to vote *en bloc* as members of a "protected" group. The 104th Congress had had thirty-eight black members of the House of Representatives under racial gerrymandering; with six fewer majority-black districts, the 105th has thirty-seven. The only black representative who didn't return as a result of the rulings was Cleo Fields, who decided not to run when his Louisiana district was invalidated. Connecticut Republican Gary Franks was defeated in an 88 percent white district, but that had nothing to do with voting rights litigation, and, for racial headcounters, it was offset by black Democrat Julia Carson's 53 percent victory over a white opponent in a 69 percent white Indianapolis district.

Redistricted black incumbents who chose to test the presumption of white bigotry by facing majority-white electorates found their courage rewarded. White "crossover" voting for blacks was clearest in Georgia, where Sanford Bishop (whose 52 percent black VRA district was displaced by one that was 35 percent black) won with 54 percent of the vote. When the Supreme Court nixed Cynthia McKinney's 60 percent black, Atlanta-to-Savannah district in 1995, she complained that black officeholders faced "extinction" and was adored as a martyr at the Harvard/*New Yorker* "Plessy v. Ferguson" conference a few months before the 1996 elections. But she won her new, 65 percent white district with 58 percent of the vote. In northern Florida, Corinne Brown (her electorate down from 55 to 42 percent black) won 61 percent of the vote.

In Texas, two black women—Democrats Sheila Jackson Lee of Houston and Eddie Bernice Johnson of Dallas—won reelection against multiple opponents in districts that had been reconfigured by court rulings to contain fewer black voters. Actually, their former black constituents had been replaced mainly by Mexican Americans, not by whites; still, their districts were a little bit whiter and a lot less black. So it's remarkable that Lee, whose constituency had gone from 51 percent black to 42 percent black, won 77 percent of the vote against three opponents, and that Johnson (whose district went down from 51 to 44 percent black), won 55 percent of the vote against five opponents, two of them fellow Democrats.

Why didn't the supposed "ethnic cleansing" occur? Because, as liberal activists refused to acknowledge, the landmark Voting Rights Act was never at risk in the Court rulings; only the advocates' subsequent, ill-advised amendments to it were at risk. The racial districting fiasco was a dramatic departure from the original act's intent and is an example of civil rights law that heightens racial divisions without proving discrimination. It's the kind of overreaching the Court began rejecting in 1993—and which liberals defended unthinkingly because it had become their status quo: "Right now, two things can change the situation," Selwyn Carter of the Southern Regional Council told the *Village Voice* in June 1996 after the Court invalidated the Texas districts. "We could get a new Supreme Court justice who supports democratic values. [Or] minority voters . . . can begin to mobilize." He, other activists, and liberal editorialists missed a third option: Enough white voters could "support democratic values" strongly enough to cross racial lines.

It was a big thing to miss. A June 1996 *New York Times* editorial accused the Court of ignoring the "inescapable fact that racially polarized voting makes it hard to elect minority candidates in majority-white districts." Yet it was millions of white voters, not advocates and judges, who had also made L. Douglas Wilder the governor of Virginia and Carol Moseley-Braun a senator from Illinois; who had elected a dozen blacks as the mayors of big, majority-white cities; and who had sent Andrew Young, Alan Wheat, Ron Dellums, Harold Ford, J. C. Watts, Gary Franks, and Julia Carson to the House from majority-white districts since 1972—all without voting rights litigation. Voters, not judges, had been telling liberals to stop making official what should be shameful—defining one's citizenship mainly by color.

One might expect that activists and journalists who believed that white voters were so ineradicably racist that black Americans could be elected only with state-mandated gerrymandering would be delighted to find it unnecessary in 1996. But for people who are chasing mirages of racial destiny, constantly on the lookout for racist threats to quicken their steps, good news can be bad news: The Court's reintegration of politics must be "segregation," and blacks' victories at the hands of white voters spell a kind of defeat. The NAACP, the ACLU, the *Times* editorial board, and other organizations and newspapers didn't celebrate the 1996 victories. "I must confess I was surprised," the ACLU's McDonald told me a few days after the election, "but it is a mistake to rely on anecdotes to show that voting is no longer polarized." The NAACP's Penda Hair said that she would have to study exit polls and counts of registered voters by race before deciding what the results meant. But no sifting of the results could deny the obvious: Even if every black voter in the Georgia and Florida districts had gone to the polls in 1996, and most whites had stayed home, Bishop, McKinney, and Brown would still have to have gotten a lot of white votes to win as they did in these majority-white districts. In fact, the white turnout in all three districts was *higher* than the black.

Disoriented by the decline in racially polarized voting, some VRA-district defenders argued that the black members' victories actually proved racial gerrymandering was essential. Without it, McDonald and Hair claimed, the victors would never have become incumbents in the first place, and so wouldn't have had the standing and track records white voters found credible in 1996. The NAACP's Theodore Shaw, who had predicted that congressional blacks would be able to fit into a taxicab, told the *New York Times*, "There was a question in my mind whether incumbency would trump race, and it appears that it has." Before the election, neither Shaw nor other voting rights activists had posed that question, much less expressed the hope that incumbency would give the redistricted blacks a fighting chance with nonblack voters; all, except David Bositis of the Joint Center for Political and Economic Studies, had announced that they would lose.

As soon as some of the redistricted incumbents surprised observers by winning the 1996 Democratic primaries in their new districts, the old, invalidated districts were touted as having powered their victories. After Cynthia McKinney and Sanford Bishop won the Georgia primaries in July, *Atlanta Journal-Constitution* editor Cynthia Tucker wrote that the Supreme Court's rulings "accidentally . . . handed them a more suitable kind of affirmative action: a foot in the door and no more. Given majority-black districts for only one election cycle, [they had] the chance to prove themselves. . . . Affirmative action programs of that kind tend to be less divisive because they do not guarantee equal success, only equal opportunity." That's nice; but even nicer—and, therefore, unnoted by voting rights activists—is the truth that if incumbency helped blacks win white majorities in areas they'd never represented before, then something fairly ordinary *does* count more than race. The redistricted blacks "weren't incumbents in *these* districts. These were new districts," voting-rights analyst Abigail Thernstrom told the *Times*. Besides, the list of blacks, like Indiana's newly elected representative Julia Carson, who were winning without being incumbents in the offices they sought, is growing. So another lesson of 1996 is that while racial bloc voting persists and should not be dismissed out of hand, neither should we dismiss cross-racial victories as aberrations. We should be studying them as precedents.

Still another is that, even if the old VRA districts were a kind of affirmative action, they were inappropriate in ways workplace affirmative action may not be. Elected officials are more than public employees, and voters are more than employers: Each elected official is "hired" not by an individual or company but by a diverse collection of citizens with varied commitments, views, and whims. Even if workplace hiring can be micromanaged by affirmative action, political sovereignty can't be, for it is ultimately about freedom, including the freedom to make bad decisions. A democracy that relies on civic virtue makes voting rights activists uneasy, because they think only in terms of supposedly monolithic and undifferentiated racial groups: "Even when minority representatives can be elected from districts that are not majority black, they cannot be as effective if they find themselves serving two masters," activist Anita Hodgkiss told David Grann, writing for the *New Republic*. That puzzled voting analyst Jerry Skurnik. "I always thought representatives had *thousands* of masters," he said.

Once every citizen has an equal vote on a basis that doesn't prejudge his or her commitments or views, everything else is up to the politics of persuasion. If citizens are bigoted or reckless in the voting booth, government can't stop them, because, at least on election day, they *are* the government. Ultimately, civic virtue and the democratic arts must be cultivated in and by the people, not imposed by self-appointed monitors. When the NAACP Legal Defense Fund, its Puerto Rican analogue, and other groups insist otherwise, they are not "civil rights" organizations, as the media call them, but ethnic-advocacy groups.

Understanding this danger, the early civil rights movement refused to write off all white voters as racists. It reached out to them, even as it challenged them. The final lesson of 1996 is that that politics of persuasion still works and that there is more civic virtue in the people than their would-be keepers assume. "The State must follow and not lead the character and progress of the citizen," wrote Ralph Waldo Emerson in his essay "Politics"; ". . . the form of government which prevails is the expression of what cultivation exists in the population which permits it. The law is only a memorandum."

♦ Ideologues, Ethnocentrists, Moralists, and Opportunists

Why can't activists on the right or the left grasp Emerson's insight? The answers are rooted in leftist ideology, black ethnocentrism, white racial moralism (driven by guilt), and simple partisan opportunism among both Republicans and Democrats.

Leftist Ideology

The racial districting story began partly in the odysseys of leftist lawyers who got into the race business to make black "empowerment" drive "progressive" economic change. In their view, oppressed and excluded blacks bear not only special wounds but a special social wisdom. Dr. King and John Lewis bore that wisdom, and they, too, wanted to mobilize it in the struggle against economic as well as racial divisions. At the 1963 March for Jobs and Freedom in Washington, D.C., King characterized constitutional guarantees of liberty as a kind of "promissory note" which blacks had come, at last, to cash. "We refuse to believe that the bank of justice is bankrupt," he added, putting liberals on the line not only politically but, as his metaphor suggested, economically.

But because he was so close to ordinary black folk and to a Christian sense of human frailty, King was realistic about the limited prospects of "overcoming" economic injustice through poor people's movements. To academic leftist analysts, by contrast, who were breezier and at the same time more dogmatic because they were more distant from the ground, aggrieved blacks are the vanguard of revolutionary change. In their view, a capitalist society must marginalize some of its population in a "reserve army of the unemployed" whose desperation keeps wages down. Thus, they say, capitalists employ racism to push blacks into that "army," giving white America a continuing rationale for *somebody's* permanent marginalization. In contrast, the left champions racial equality in order to expose the fiction of white America's fantasies of an equal-opportunity society with no permanent class divisions. In this view, weaving the black thread right into the center of the social fabric, as in racial districting, isn't only the right thing to do; it's also a way to unravel the fabric itself, exposing its contradictions and lies.

Concentrating on race, not class, seems an astute tactic in a society where law addresses injustices based on race but not on class. Because law protects private property and its owners' freedom to invest or disinvest as they see fit, it cannot uproot economic inequities. So leftists, drawing upon King's and Lewis's courage, learned to charge "racism" against public officials and private corporations in court in order to destabilize the system by extracting material and political benefits for the black poor. The activist sociologist Frances Fox Piven was explicit about this in trying to flood New York's welfare rolls with hundreds of thousands of blacks and Hispanics in the 1960s, when unemployment was low; in an unwitting analogy to President Nixon's use of affirmative action to divide white-ethnic Democrats from black Democrats, Piven argued that black demands for more welfare would so anger white tax-payers, thus disrupting the Democratic coalition, that nervous liberal politicians would replace welfare with an even more ambitious guaranteed minimum income for all Americans.

For activists steeped in this tradition of using race as a proxy for class, voting rights litigation is but another front of the struggle. In their hearts and minds, though not on their lawyerly lips, the language of racial "inclusion" is a proxy for a language of economic transformation. But it is also an expression of leftist racial opportunism, for most people with dark skins want to join the system, not serve as the vanguard of an anticapitalist revolution. That is why black and white voters together helped to reelect Florida's Corinne Brown, who had proved herself a reliable provider of "pork" in military spending, and Georgia's Sanford Bishop, who looked after the interests of his "redneck" peanut farmers. However, many on the left consider such blacks the victims of "false consciousness"; civil rights attorney and former Clinton nominee for U.S. Assistant Attorney General for Civil Rights Lani Guinier did write that blacks who win in majority-white districts may not be "authentic" representatives of their people. After the 1996 elections, the ACLU's Laughlin McDonald sounded almost mournful as he told me that Sanford Bishop's "voting record is more Republican, to the right; that explains his success."

But since the law and the careers of activists like McDonald constrain them to argue in terms of race, not class, they couldn't object very loudly when, in 1996, some black politicians addressed white voters in the name of shared middle-class values and aspirations. The advocates and their Justice Department colleagues were trapped defending a racial "inclusion" that subverted their more "progressive" political agenda. Guinier was one of the few black voting rights activists to try to break out of that trap by calling for an end to *all* geographical districting and the introduction of other systems of voting that are beyond our scope here.

In fairness, voting rights liberals who aren't anticapitalist face a poignant dilemma, too: The expanding black middle class, living in mostly black suburbs and preoccupied with corporate success and consumption, is not quite what the civil rights movement's "beloved community" envisioned. Unease and even regret about this are understandable, but they hardly justify campaigns for "solutions" such as proportional racial representation.

Black Ethnocentrism

Not all blacks do want to join the capitalist system, of course. The more rudderless and valueless consumer culture becomes, the more people of all races are tempted to seek havens in subcultures rooted in a particular ethnicity, ideology, or doctrine, not markets. Blacks, so long and so harshly excluded from capitalist culture and so vulnerable to its enticements, have often felt ambivalent about joining it, even when they could. The structures of endurance and resistance they created across centuries of exclusion may not have been "progressive" in an anticapitalist sense, but they were formidable redoubts of dignity. When such structures have succumbed to the seductions of consumer marketing and government entitlements, they are often sorely missed; it can be as tempting to withdraw into folkish discipline, as Louis Farrakhan urges, as it is to seek full integration. In that sense, Farrakhan's sympathizers and Christian fundamentalists often understand one another quite well.

Black leftists are more torn, and their voting rights confusion reflects it. On the one hand, they, like Farrakhan, want blacks to deepen their solidarity against the system. On the other, as "progressives," they want blacks to integrate the system enough to join interracial coalitions that will change the system itself. But if black solidarity has decayed into little more than a collection of orchestrated insecurities, the prospect of integration can be frightening. As the writer Shelby Steele explains in *The Content of Our Character*, it brings "the shock of being suddenly accountable on strictly personal terms. [Integration shock] occurs in situations that disallow race as an excuse for personal shortcomings and it therefore exposes vulnerabilities that were previously hidden" behind postures of group defiance and withdrawal. "When one lacks the courage to face oneself fully," Steele continues, "a fear of hidden vulnerabilities triggers a fright-flight response to integration shock. Instead of admitting that racism has declined, we argue all the harder that it is still alive and more insidious than ever." Hence the search for a proportional racial representation that seems to keep blacks "authentically" black, and whites white.

But if racism is thought to be on the rise and if black identity is inherently oppositional, then victories like Corinne Brown's and Sanford Bishop's thanks to white voters must be explained away. And as long as there are enough guilt-ridden whites eager to make amends for racism, there is some apparent reward for voting rights activists' persistent claims of victimization. They can try to have it both ways: They want representation by reparation—the simulacrum of empowerment that comes with "safe" legislative seats—but not the real power and responsibility that would come from organizing and mobilizing thousands of voters. That is why turnout in the districts they create is so low, and why the districts' champions are eerily untroubled by the apathy.

White Liberal Moralism

Some of the gloomiest black racists achieve an odd serenity when they find whites who are guilt-ridden enough to defer to their otherwise nonsensical ideas. It is one of the great ironies behind incessant charges of racism: Those who condemn whites the most flamboyantly tend to be those who know that they can count on a deep reservoir of white remorse and goodwill. On the night of her 1996 Democratic primary victory in her new, majority-white district, Cynthia McKinney did have to acknowledge this. She seemed at once delighted and nonplussed: "The people of the Fourth District decided to get on board the history train!" she exulted, without specifying where she thought the train was heading. Two months later, she was back in court seeking the return of her old, majority-black district—an irony that irritated some white residents of her new district who had voted for her. The *New York Times* ran a photograph of a smiling McKinney resting her head endearingly on the shoulder of Laughlin McDonald, the ACLU voting rights lawyer who had predicted a return to the days of all-white government when the old district was invalidated. The story never mentioned that the two were trying to get McKinney out of the district that had just elected her.

Political Opportunism

If ideologues, ethnocentrists, and moralists are driven to racism by their illusions, most politicians are drawn to it by opportunism. In public controversies over important principles, most politicians are moral dilettantes: When they see narrow political opportunities in moral posturing, they take them. Republican operatives who helped liberal Democrats create the majority-minority districts in some states saw an opportunity to escape from the Democratic habit of packing Republicans into a few GOP districts while spreading blacks, who are usually Democrats, into mostly white districts, giving white Democrats an edge against Republicans.

As we have seen, the original VRA had already stopped some of these practices, enabling real black and Hispanic communities to send candidates of their choice to Congress. But now that the 1982 amendments to the act had made race as important a factor as partisan gain and were packing even geographically dispersed minorities into special districts, the adjacent white districts could become whiter and, potentially, more susceptible to "us versus them" appeals by Republicans. The GOP had avoided such talk when its representatives had had black or Hispanic constituents. Now, they made race a "wedge issue" to divide and regroup the electorate along partisan lines. Since districting is almost inherently partisan, no one could blame Republicans for grabbing any legal tool to counteract years of Democratic-run districting. Still, the GOP's embrace of racial gerrymandering was cynical. For years, the administrations of Ronald Reagan and George Bush had denounced racial quotas and proportionalism. Now, the Bush Justice Department had helped racial advocacy groups draw districts pursuant to the 1982 amendments.

Activists who believed that minority "empowerment" would come from corraling blacks and Hispanics into special districts should have sensed their own tactical, if not philosophical, blunder when they started getting logistical and financial support from conservative foundations and Republican Party operatives. But black politicians seeking more "safe" seats for themselves and their colleagues got greedy. "I'm not going to sacrifice a black district to be a Democrat. I was black before I was a Democrat," Kay Patterson, a South Carolina state senator who chaired that legislature's Black Caucus, told the conservative journalist Peter Brown. Such thinking made possible the hypocritical collaboration of voting rights activists and Republicans—"the ultimate political one-night stand," Brown called it, knowing who'd feel "had" by morning: In 1994, the newly whitened districts helped Republicans win Congress. As the Supreme Court began to invalidate the new minority-majority districts that had made this possible, Republicans fell silent for a while and seemed to acknowledge their hypocrisy. But early in 1997, former Republican National Committee counsel Benjamin Ginsberg told representatives of black civil rights groups at a Washington conference that a good deal of racial districting remains possible under the new Court strictures and that the advocates' "best deal will again be with Republicans."

But will the Democrats hop back into bed with Republicans

when redistricting resumes in 2001? White Democrats who had backed the '82 amendments found themselves out of office after losing their nonwhite constituents. The Congressional Black Caucus grew by nine members, but it found itself more isolated in a Republican-run legislature, stripped of its powerful House committee chairmanships. Will they now forswear racial districting, even if it means losing a few "black" seats, in order to regain Democratic control of the House?

Long before the VRA was enacted, Democrats bargained ethnically and racially. They created urban machines that preached "the American Way" while catering to loyalists along carefully patrolled ethnic and racial lines. In a sense, the 1982 VRA amendments merely ratcheted up this unofficial practice into a legally mandated formula. But there is something to be said for the old, informal balancing of ethnic and "American" loyalties. Because it did not make racial or ethnic identity the official foundation of public policy, this balancing offered more incentive for such graduates of the old ethnic spoils systems as Barbara Jordan and Mario Cuomo to transcend their parochial ethnic and racial origins and affirm the American faith to which Lyndon Johnson had appealed from the House podium in 1965. But as proportional racial representation cost such Democrats white support, it left them more dependent on keeping black and Hispanic activists and politicos happy, even if that meant encouraging Balkanization.

Some have learned better since 1994 and again since 1996, when, ironically, Supreme Court rulings against racial districting shifted some of Cynthia McKinney's and Sanford Bishop's former black constituents back into neighboring white districts. The Republicans there were reelected but by smaller margins, and they may now be more responsive to blacks' concerns. Most liberal Democrats I spoke with acknowledged that racial districting had been a disaster. But the black incumbents among them were trapped in their short-run gains, even if not in racial loyalty or ideology—trapped, that is, until the voters liberated them almost despite themselves.

Since good racial news discomfits those who tout racial victimization, messengers bringing good news can't be endured.

In 1982, two lobbyists for the VRA amendments told Abigail Thernstrom, the critic of racial districting, "If you testify against the amendments, we will blacklist you with every politician and voting rights lawyer you want to interview for your book." Although her *Whose Votes Count?* won four impressive awards from organizations such as the American Bar Association, a review by University of Virginia law professor Pamela Karlan and voting rights activist Peyton McCrary claimed that it "so distorts the evidence that it cannot be taken seriously as scholarship." The liberal Twentieth Century Fund, which sponsored the book, forgot to list it among all its other books in a seventy-fifth anniversary publication.

"We need electoral arrangements that deliver the right messages," Thernstrom wrote in the *Washington Post* in 1991. "And the right messages are: that we are all Americans, that we're in this together, that the government thinks of us and treats us as individual citizens with individual (not group) rights, that whites can represent blacks and blacks can represent whites, that we have no need for legislative quotas, since distinct racial and ethnic groups are not nations in our society. . . ." Her essay, entitled "A Republican–Civil Rights Conspiracy," condemned both sides for betraying that vision.

Liberal voting-rights activists dismissed Thernstrom's words as naively ahistorical or, worse, as pieties covering racism. But in 1996, the words took on an historic ring. "I am not your African-American candidate; I am the Democratic candidate for Congress," said Indiana's Julia Carson on the eve of her victory in a heavily white congressional district, sounding the winning note that unnerves liberal racists because it reverses their view of the world.

Ethnocentric activists, their conservative collaborators, and others who have supported racial districting need a new language that begins with three simple words: "We were wrong." They were wrong about the intent and spirit of the Voting Rights Act. They were wrong about the Supreme Court's rulings against using race as the dominant factor in districting. They were wrong about messengers of the good news that Americans will reward something better; indeed, they were wrong about the voters themselves. And they are still wrong, because their unspoken goal remains not integration but proportional racial representation that has no place in an America that is overcoming its racism, past and present.

I first understood that racial destiny is a fantasy as I watched Lyndon Johnson say, "We *shall* overcome," and realized that he had been driven to say it by the moral example of John Lewis and Martin Luther King, Jr. Lewis was right to say, during the 1992 reapportionment, that when he defied Selma's Sheriff Clark he was hoping "to create an interracial democracy in America . . . not separate racial enclaves," and that the VRA's purpose should be "to create a climate in which people of color will have an opportunity to represent . . . all Americans." He risked his life for that vision; King lost his life for it. In the 1996 elections, unsung heroes in voting booths instructed those who were sliding away from that vision not to give up on it. What they should give up on instead are their fantasies of racial destiny.

CHAPTER 4

MEDIA MYOPIA

◆ What's at Stake

One *New York Times* reporter who covered the voting rights marches in Selma in 1965 was the future bestselling author Gay Talese, whose *The Kingdom and the Power* is a history of that paper. In March 1990, when civil rights leaders returned to Selma to mark the twenty-fifth anniversary of the marches, Talese got the *Times* to send him back, too, to describe how the town had changed since Sheriff Clark's billy clubs had prompted Lyndon Johnson's "We *shall* overcome." Talese learned that Randall Miller, a black man who had taken injured marchers to the hospital in 1965, was now the city's personnel director, and that, on the day when Selma would commemorate the marches, Miller would marry a white woman in an integrated gathering and neighborhood within earshot of the public ceremonies.

Talese and a *Times* photographer covered the wedding with the couple's permission, photographing them and Selma's mayor to produce vivid testimony to profound racial change. The *Times* published Talese's account, beginning on page 1, but not the wedding photo, which, Talese learned, a black editor had objected to running. Years later, at a symposium on the media, Talese asked the paper's assistant managing editor, Gerald Boyd, whether it was he who'd dropped the photo, and, if so, why. Boyd replied that he had opposed running the picture, because, he said, it was "boring. . . . To show an integrated couple on the front page wasn't news. The picture didn't represent anything new."

"In *Selma?*" Talese asked incredulously. Boyd stuck to his argument.

"I didn't feel he was being candid," Talese told me later. "I grew up in the North but attended the University of Alabama from 1949 to 1953, and what I saw in those four years was a separate country, a different America. It was still that way in 1965, when I went to Selma for the *Times*. We all bring our own experiences to what we write; there's no such thing as purely objective reporting. But here, I thought this man's judgment was just wrong. I mean, to see this couple hand in hand, with no Klan outside the door, not far from the Edmund Pettus Bridge [where the marchers were confronted by state troopers], well, that says *something*."

Not to everyone, it doesn't. For some, "good" racial news implies more progress than they would like. What may strike whites as progress may not be welcomed by blacks: Some may dislike racial integration in adoptions, sexual relations, and matrimony, for example, tolerating it as the private choice of individuals, yet resenting it as a betrayal of black pride.

Boyd denies having been uncomfortable in any of these ways. At an International Press Freedom Awards ceremony late in 1996, Talese felt a tap on his shoulder, turned, and saw a smiling Boyd say, "I didn't do what you think I did"— meaning (in Talese's estimation, since Boyd didn't elaborate) that he had vetoed the photo, but not for any "racial" reason. But, with all due respect to whatever Boyd's feelings about highlighting the marriage may have been, such a photo in the *Times* would indeed have been striking. Given millions of Americans' memories and hopes, the marriage *was* a cultural, even historic, event. The *Times* would have been wrong to withhold it in deference to anyone's discomfort with interracial marriage. (At one time, such a photo would have been withheld in deference to segregationists' discomfort.)

Talese couldn't shake his doubts about the decision because he had come to feel that the *Times* deferred too often to a new liberal racism. At the symposium he complained that the paper's news reporting was too "correct" and often lacked "a sense of reality." This matters, for the *Times* is the cerebrum of national print and broadcast journalism: Every evening at around 9 PM, Eastern Time, the first edition of the next day's paper is delivered or faxed to editors at other newspapers and to senior producers of network television news departments around the world. The *Times* helps them to decide what to select as "news that's fit to print" from the day's torrent of voices and events, and what to publicize "without fear or favor"—as the paper's own mottoes put it. Talese's *and* Boyd's discomfort over the photograph demonstrates the high stakes at which even relatively unimportant decisions are made.

Also influential are the *Times*'s own opinions about people and events, presented in editorials that are the paper's "official," institutional voice, and in essays written by half a dozen *Times* columnists on the "op-ed" (short for "opposite the editorial") pages. At issue here is not only *what* positions the *Times* takes on controversial issues, but also *how* it takes them: The most constructive way to debate an issue in an open society is to take one's opponents' best arguments into account, for the goal is not to score points, as student debaters do, but to find intellectually and politically viable solutions to real problems. Doing that in editorials requires intelligent thinking and persuasion, not cheap shots or intimidation.

Every news medium must earn its audience's trust every day. Like the pope, after all, the *Times* has no troops to make anyone defer to its judgments. Its credibility depends ultimately on the respect accorded it by readers who are active in civic life, politics, industry, the arts, and in a shared, if complicated, national civic culture. *Times* editorials affirm these readers' integrity by serving up smart insights and sound arguments upon which busy and powerful people depend, and by articulating standards by which they are willing to be called to account. Readers want to be informed and persuaded, not peppered with propaganda or cheaply shamed.

Yet even the cerebrum of a strong national community is but a fragile craft in history's tides; it can drift, lose course, and founder. A growing number and variety of observers, writing in publications as diverse as the *Columbia Journalism Review*, the *Forbes Media Critic*, the *San Francisco Chronicle*, and the *Washington Post*, have been complaining that the *Times*'s cultural and political coverage has become less responsible in the ways I've just mentioned and too much in harness to assumptions that ought to be subject to more debate in its pages. They charge that *Times* reportage and commentary are skewed by racial and sexual groupthink—by a "diversity" mind-set that hobbles good journalism because it lacks "a sense of reality," as Talese put it.

The old *Times* could be narrow and flawed, but at least it was grounded in classical liberal principles that emphasized individuals' rights, empirically based rational analysis, and, with these, a healthy skepticism about the pronouncements and policies of anyone in power. The "old" journalism was sometimes deferential and sentimental toward established power and custom, but its humanist principles made it sensitive to injustices the civil rights and anti–Vietnam War movements exposed and quick to spot obfuscation and obstruction. The same principles make good journalists skeptical of even insurgent groups or movements, which, as they grow in power, are prone to obfuscate and obstruct. When the gains of the civil rights and other social "revolutions" are institutionalized—as in racial districting for "voting rights"—it may not be long before the classical liberal principles to which those revolutions appealed are abused, betraying even the supposedly "empowered." Good journalists are not crusaders or missionaries. Their job is to uncover the truth, even when it hurts.

◆ What Wasn't Fit to Print

By the mid-1990s, observers like Talese suspected that a new *Times* mind-set was enforcing an unfeeling obeisance to liberal racial myths that are corrosive of true liberal principles, and, with them, of freedom. That disquieting shift, the subject of this chapter, was all too evident in the *Times*'s commentary and coverage of the 1996 voting rights controversies—a stark illustration not only of liberals' misplaced moralism, ethnocentrism, and opportunism, but also of the media's astonishing deference to them.

As the Supreme Court began to invalidate congressional districts shaped more by race than by the usual partisan line-drawing, *Times* editorials and even news coverage reinforced the civil rights establishment's belief that challenges to racial districts foretold a return to the segregationist past. Editorial after editorial accused the justices of using "topsy-turvy logic" that "could start a second post-Reconstruction movement in American politics, strangling fledgling efforts to secure a more integrated national legislature" (December 24, 1994). In a 1993 ruling, according to the *Times*, Justice Sandra Day O'Connor practiced "Jurassic Park jurisprudence" by posing hard questions about racial districting and ordering a lower court to hear arguments against a convoluted majority-black district in North Carolina.

By 1996, this inability to consider other obvious explanations had become a *dis*ability. When the Supreme Court invalidated racial districting in Texas, bringing to seven the number of "majority-minority" districts it had struck down, a *Times* editorial cried, "One hundred years after the Supreme Court's decision in *Plessy v. Ferguson* set back the cause of racial justice by approving a doctrine of 'separate but equal,' a majority of the current Court members have demonstrated a perverse determination to resegregate the nation's politics. A century from now, fair-minded Americans are bound to view the Court's evisceration of the Voting Rights Act this week with regret and even shame" (June 6, 1996).

Actually, as we saw in the last chapter, it took fair-minded

Americans less than six months to return a true verdict on the effect of racial redistricting, by reelecting five black incumbents who'd moved to new, majority-white districts. The only people with occasion for shame turned out to be those voting rights officials, activists, and editorial writers who endorsed using race as the dominant factor in districting. But far more surprising than the *Times*'s myopia about this was its stark malfeasance in refusing to acknowledge the results. Its election coverage simply didn't report or comment on the momentous victories by blacks whose old districts had been eliminated by the rulings the paper had protested so loudly. Only after I had called attention to the *Times*'s silence in the *New Republic* did it run a news story, on a Saturday, about the victories. The story was thorough, balanced—and three weeks late.

The editorial page remained silent: "Journalists are prone to vanity, and we do like to think of ourselves as threats to power and foolishness," editorial-page editor Howell Raines has written. Apparently, after the 1996 elections, it was he who felt threatened. Six months before the election, Raines had emphasized the importance of challenging conventional wisdom in his critique of the journalist James Fallows's argument in *Breaking the News*, that reporters should spend less time chasing "horse-race" election stories and more time working with communities to improve public debate and civic consensus. "[The] wisdom of democracy is forged in the rowdy ceremonies of the campaign trail and . . . unrestrained debate," Raines retorted, and "the participation of mainstream print journalists in this process as skeptical observers, critics and analysts is a high, venerable and independent calling. . . ." Raines saw an "insidious danger when reporters and editors become public-policy missionaries with a puritanical contempt for horse-race politics."

Yet when the rowdy ceremonies of the campaign trail forged a new wisdom about racial districting, the *Times* opinion pages suppressed all debate. Before the elections, no ruling against racial districting had escaped Raines's denunciation. After them, the editorial page never mentioned, much less applauded, the "fair-minded Americans" who, oblivious of doomsaying, had reelected black incumbents. No essay submitted to the op-ed page on the subject was published. *Times* columnists ducked, too. Before the elections, Anthony Lewis had warned that "the reality in the South is that black men and women, however well qualified, have little chance of winning in white districts." After the elections, Lewis said nothing at all.

The *Times* remained silent a few months later, when, in its own backyard, the federal court in New York's Eastern District invalidated the "Hispanic" 12th Congressional District. There was no editorial. There were no op-ed pieces. There were news stories on the decision, but the *Times* did not report any interview with Angel Diaz, the lead plaintiff (see Chapter 3) who Representative Velazquez now charged was a "puppet" of right-wing conservatives. Perhaps liberal racism led reporters to take her word for it, to assume that an Hispanic Republican in a poor Brooklyn neighborhood must be someone's inarticulate dupe. Only *Newsday* editorial writer Joseph Dolman bothered to call Diaz and report that the plaintiff had a mind of his own.

Once again, the *Times* was functioning more as a social policy missionary than as a newspaper. Its "social and political values are easily discerned in its pages," noted *Washington Post* ombudsman Richard Harwood in a column commenting on Raines's essay about Fallows. And the perils of a liberal racist mind-set are all the more dangerous when its very existence is denied. "People get notions of how Machiavellian the *Times* is," Susan Rasky, a former staffer there, told *San Francisco Examiner* media critic David Armstrong. "It's a big, lumbering machine; it wouldn't *know* how to be politically correct." But the problem is not a Machiavellian conspiracy; it is the subtle transformation of editors' and reporters' thinking by unspoken assumptions that gain ground at a paper as they do in the liberal professional social stratum from which its journalists increasingly come.

The *Times* is hardly the progenitor of liberal disdain for ordinary people of all colors, but its prestige and its pose as a defender of helpless blacks against oppressive white majorities serve to chill reasonable criticism of outlandish racial assumptions. In 1991, when Arthur Sulzberger, Jr., inherited the publisher's office from his politically more moderate father, he announced that news would no longer be viewed only from a "white, male, and straight" perspective. Whether there *is* such a perspective in most news ought to have been debated, not assumed. "Arthur keeps talking about the day being long past when the news will be told only through the straight, white, male point of view," a *Times* reporter told the journalist Robert Sam Anson for *Esquire* magazine. "Who is this white male? Adolf Hitler? Albert Schweitzer? Me?" Who, for that matter, are black males? Asian females? The answers are not as simple as they seem in the news coverage and commentary of most liberal media.

◆ Diversity's Rich Ironies

To understand how the characteristic *Times* mind-set gets race wrong, consider a pair of columns by Frank Rich, the paper's former theater critic, whom Sulzberger has hand-picked to review the theater of politics on the op-ed page under editorial-page editor Raines's supervision. In an October 18, 1995 column about the Million Man March entitled "Fixated on Farrakhan," Rich condemned Louis Farrakhan but was even more emphatic about the underlying social causes of his rise:

> The pre-march attacks on Mr. Farrakhan did nothing to deter 400,000 African-Americans, only a minority of whom support the Nation of Islam, from turning up in Washington to express their impassioned desire to stem the economic and social collapse of their own communities. . . . By continuing to fixate on Mr. Farrakhan, rather than the legitimate concerns of the 400,000 marchers, white politicians only give their nemesis more credibility and power. It is the failure of the entire political establishment to heed the spiraling crisis of the black underclass in the

first place that gave the extremist Mr. Farrakhan his opening to seize a resonant mainstream issue as his own.

This admonition to hear the dissatisfied, not the demagogue, was a legitimate contribution to public debate. Although Rich didn't mention it, Newt Gingrich had said much the same thing, opining to TV talk-show host Larry King that if blacks' level of pain was so great that only a Farrakhan could speak to it, politicians ought to pay heed. What was wrong in Rich's mind-set was clear a year later, when he wrote about a "mostly white million man march" which, he reported, is coalescing under the aegis of Promise Keepers, an evangelical men's movement, one of whose rallies he had attended at Shea Stadium. This time, he reversed his emphasis completely, fixating on the supposed demagogues, not the dissatisfied. The latter he dispatched as follows: "During a marathon rally of sermonizing, singing and praying, the [35,000 men at Shea] also repeatedly sobbed and hugged each other—or, more joyously, slapped high-fives while repeating the chant, 'Thank God I'm a man!' " (September 25, 1996).

How many actually sobbed while hugging one another is unclear in Rich's column, but Rafael Olmeda, the *Daily News* reporter quoted in Chapter 1 who covered the Shea Stadium rally, told me that most of the behavior resembled that at Farrakhan's event, which also had tears, hugs, high-fives, and elements of religious revival. More troubling was Rich's failure to report that the stadium crowd was about 25 percent black and Hispanic and that whites and nonwhites greeted and sat next to one another as individuals. Perhaps because he shares Sulzberger's belief that "We're all going to have to understand [our racial and sexual] differences, be aware of them, know what they mean, understand that we don't all see the world . . . the same way," Rich did not report or comment on what Promise Keepers founder Bill McCartney, who is white but the grandfather of two interracial children, told the rally: A "spirit of white racial superiority," warned McCartney, deepens "insensitivity to the pain of people of color."

Because Rich saw the crowd as white, he did not detect any

"impassioned desire to stem the economic and social collapse" of *these* men's communities. Many at Promise Keepers rallies have endured family breakdown, driven in part by economic and cultural upheavals that leave them feeling materially and emotionally bereft. Rich sneered at them. "The Promise Keepers I met at Shea seemed more motivated by a Robert Blyesque hunger to overcome macho inhibitions and reconnect with God than by any desire to enlist in a political army. But an army PK [Promise Keepers] most certainly is."

Having caricatured the men at Shea, Rich devoted most of his column to the rally's organizers, whose counterparts at Farrakhan's march he had all but ignored:

> Alfred Ross, who researched Planned Parenthood's early, pre-Oklahoma City warnings about the militia movement, says that PK is the heir to Jerry Falwell's Moral Majority and Pat Robertson's Christian Coalition as "the third wave of the religious right's assault on American democracy and values"—a view he airs in the current issue of *The Nation*. The journalist Fred Clarkson writes . . . that PK is "the most dynamic element of the Christian right of the mid 1990s" and "a front and recruiting agency" for its political ambitions.
>
> These and other critics cite PK's anti-feminist call for men to "take back" power from women, its cult-like psychology and its authoritarian, military-modeled organization, with its proliferating network of local cells. Particularly ominous are the many ideological and financial links between the PK hierarchy and organizations that are pushing the full religious-right agenda of outlawing abortion, demonizing homosexuals, and bringing prayer and the teaching of creationism to public schools.

This agenda is the same as Louis Farrakhan's, of course; the Nation of Islam is nothing if not cultlike and military modeled. At Shea, the *News*'s Olmeda saw and spoke with liberal black and Hispanic pastors from Brooklyn and the Bronx. "They're against abortion," he told me, "but that's as far right as they go. The closest thing to a demagogue I saw was Chuck Colson, and neither he nor anyone else said a word about politics, except to say that the event crossed all political and racial lines." What Rich encountered at Shea was a mass of people who reject many of his beliefs, as did many on the Washington Mall the year before. Back then, Rich's sensitivity to black suffering numbed his reaction to the demagoguery on the podium; now, no such inhibition blocked him from taking alarm at a demagoguery he thought he saw, in white-face, at Shea. He ended his Promise Keepers column with a warning:

> The mainstream media . . . mainly cover PK as a human-interest story. But if the press was right (and it was) to ask how the leader of the last, black Million Man March might exploit that event's honorable goals and participants for his own insidious political aims, surely it's past time to apply the same scrutiny to a mostly white million man march of equally controversial provenance and potentially far greater political force.

The disingenuous twist here is that, actually, the media had covered the Million Man March mainly as a benign human interest story, not an occasion to probe Farrakhan's exploitation. Rich had warned the media not to "fixate" on how Farrakhan might manipulate the event for his own insidious aims but to focus instead on the yearnings of the men in attendance. Again, that is fair. But there were similar yearnings at Shea, and Rich didn't mention them. And since he is a perceptive fellow, such an omission can have but one explanation: His liberal racism determined what he could bring himself to observe and report.

Rich missed yet another development relevant to these rallies, but, then, so did every other commentator at every other liberal publication in the United States. Two days after O. J. Simpson's acquittal divided the nation, and ten days before Americans were riveted by Farrakhan's march, Pope John Paul II led hundreds of thousands of worshippers of all colors at masses in an inner-city cathedral, a racetrack, and a sports stadium in New Jersey and New York. The *Times* covered the visit lavishly, yet no editorial or column after the Farrakhan march assessed or even noted the remarkable contrasts between it and the racially integrated outpouring of social and religious faith led by the pope. Racial groupthink and "religio-phobia" denied some journalists a full awareness of what was unfolding before them under the aegis of a Roman Catholic Church that, *mirabile dictu,* had become one of racial inte-gration's best hopes.

My point is not that journalists should applaud the Church but that they should ponder the ironies in its influence. What does it mean to Frank Rich and the *New York Times* that the Archie and Edith Bunkers whom the pope led in prayer might well have flocked to the polls to support Colin Powell had he become the Republican presidential nominee against Bill Clinton? What does it mean to Rich and the *Times* that of the five Catholic high schools built in northern Manhattan at the start of this century, when the area's population was white, all five are still operating and sending disproportionate numbers of their poor black and Hispanic graduates on to college, while other religious institutions moved on as the area's ethnic and racial composition changed? If news features, editorials, and columns are evidence, these things mean nothing at all.

Nothing Rich has written suggests that he sees the Catholic Church as anything but a redoubt of sexism, homophobia, and priestly obscurantism. Show him masses of white-ethnic men yearning together with blacks and Hispanics, and, some-how, he sees militias forming. As a columnist, he is entitled to his opinions. My point is that his columns explicate the mind-set that governs *Times* coverage of the news under Sulz-berger. Such is the paper's distance from ordinary New Yorkers, and, indeed, most Americans, that few who attended the Shea Stadium rally would have read Rich's column about it, and anyone who did would have found himself portrayed as a rather dangerous fellow or a dupe, preoccupied with "macho" predilections and sexist fears.

Most *Times* coverage of political and social movements and trends isn't as pointed and accusatory as Rich's. Yet much of it assumes and ignores what he assumes and ignores. Any reporter who is unlucky enough to view the world as smugly and myopically as Rich does—and, remember, he is Sulzberger's choice for an important columnist's perch—is going to miss or mischaracterize people who are decent but different in ways that don't conform to approved and internalized notions of "diversity."

◆ Mindless Diversity

How can such a mind-set get hold of journalists, who are skeptical and irreverent by nature? One answer is that mind-sets come in handy under pressure. Plunged daily into a torrent of actors and events out of which they must make some sense on a deadline, journalists use whatever story lines or narratives are already in their heads or easily at hand. All of us do this, but journalists are supposed to interview strangers with strange beliefs and take leaps of social and moral imagination to explain what they see. A journalist's best asset is a mind well trained and furnished by liberal education—the kind of mind Harvard Law School professor Randall Kennedy characterizes as "animated by a liberal, individualistic, and universal ethos which is skeptical of . . . the particularisms— national, ethnic, religious, and racial—which seem to have grown so strong recently. . . ."

When pressures to impose certain racial and sexual story lines come not only from home or the street but from managers hell-bent on reforming a newspaper itself, some journalists will adopt the quasi-official mind-set as a matter of both convenience and conviction. They will do it about as thoroughly as their predecessors adopted and internalized the institutional racism of white-male newsrooms, where liberals of goodwill believed (or kept telling themselves) that they were standard-bearers of justice. Journalists at conservative papers such as the *New York Post* and the *Washington Times* adopt mind-sets, too. It is bad enough that most of us become creatures of habit as we age, but it is sadder to see bright young reporters closed off to freedom of thought.

Times editorials and news stories about racial, sexual, and other cultural controversies often read as if they were hatched in corporate management seminars that conscript simplistic notions of identity into battles for bigger market shares. Sulzberger believes that "managed diversity" is as good for business as it is for social redemption. "Diversity is the single most important issue facing this paper," he has said. "If we were only doing this to change the paper and not to make money, then it legitimately would be a harder thing to do. But I don't think we have a problem here. . . ." But he does have a problem. To reconcile its corporate bottom line with "diversity training" and multicultural news coverage, a newspaper has to caricature individuals and the subcultures to which they may or may not belong.

"Managed diversity is even bigger than affirmative action," Sulzberger says. It is not enough just to hire a more racially and sexually varied workforce, he says. The company must embrace that variety "through training. We are all going to have to understand those differences, be aware of them, know what they mean, understand that we don't all see the world . . . in the same way. . . . Managed diversity is about changing the way we view each other and the way we view the news. . . . You can see it reflected in the pages of the paper every day."

Americans certainly don't all see the world in the same way. But neither do they like to think that their differences run unerringly along racial and sexual group lines, as opposed to, say, individual, religious, class, or geographical lines. Part of the story of every racial and ethnic group that has entered the United States in significant numbers—from Anglo-Saxon Protestants to the latest Chinese immigrants—is bitter exploitation or repression by members of its own group, even in America. Yet the *Times* too often assumes that the racial and sexual differences are the important ones, and, like Frank Rich at Shea Stadium, it is inclined to report that they are, even when they aren't.

For ample historical reasons, black people do tend to express themselves along racial-group lines in opinion polls more often than do Hispanics, Asians, and even whites, but there is no good reason for news media to defer and even to

pander to that tragic tendency. The history of black racial solidarity and exceptionalism, fostering a feeling of entitlement to
play by different rules, is as old as racism itself. Yet differences
that are vital to serious undertakings, be they business ven-
tures or political movements, have little to do with cultural
differences coded by color, surname, or sex. Coding people
this way and calling it "awareness" eclipses important, race-
neutral standards and needs. Sulzberger insists that managed
diversity shakes up the white men's racist arrangements and
assumptions: "If white men weren't complaining, it would be
an indication that we weren't succeeding and making the
inroads that we are." But by labeling people much as the old
white male system did, managed diversity reinforces the
assumption that skin colors betoken profound differences.
The strategy is reductive and counterproductive, as is evident
from this note accompanying a survey report in *A Changing
Times*, the newspaper's in-house "diversity newsletter":

> An apology from the Mentoring team: Becoming more sensitive
> to and better understanding diversity is a learning process for
> all of us, and mistakes are bound to be made. We inadvertently
> overlooked "Asian" as a designated choice among the various
> ethnic groups represented. We apologize for the oversight.
> (October/November 1994)

The "mentoring team," one of twenty-three diversity action
teams which Sulzberger has "challenged and empowered . . .
to assist in the creation of a Human Resources infrastructure"
to promote "diversity" at the paper, had taken a survey to correlate employees' mentoring patterns or preferences with
their race or ethnicity. It meant to ask whether "Asian"
employees tended to have mentors and whether those mentors were "Asian," too, or of another "designated" ethnicity.
But no useful information about individual employees is con-
veyed by labels such as "Asian," "Hispanic," "Caucasian," and
"African American." For example, two years ago an Hispanic
Times reporter protested that he was being patronized by a
diversity trainer who assured him that Hispanics have "strong

family values." Which values? And who are Hispanics? Puerto Ricans in the Bronx? Mexican Americans in East Los Angeles? Cubans in Coral Gables?

Surely the word "Asian," for whose omission the mentoring team apologized, is a white imposition upon peoples as diverse as Afghanis, Pakistanis, Indians, Vietnamese, Chinese, Koreans, Japanese, and twenty others. What cultural characteristics do they share? Should editors and reporters be "aware" of such differences as they work with individuals designated as "Asian"? What if Pakistani Muslims have beliefs about family structure, women's roles, and homosexuality that are anathema to Sulzberger? What will his understanding "that we don't all see the world . . . the same way" do for *them?* Should an "Asian" reporter and a black reporter (who may be from Ghana or Baltimore) be sent together to cover an angry black boycott of Korean stores in Brooklyn? Shouldn't humanist principles count more than racialist ones in guiding a paper's coverage of a boycott that dishonors truth-telling and even civil disobedience? Diversity "is reflected in our news coverage, and in our ability to cover the news," Sulzberger says. If so, how?

And what about the impact of diversity labeling on whites in-house? Should we be "aware" of cultural differences among whites, too? If so, should we be "aware" of Sulzberger's own mixed, German-Jewish and WASP heritage? By his logic, aren't such differences also important? Shouldn't he participate in a diversity-training session with top management to air and explore them?

By mid-1996, it was clear to many that the quasi-therapeutic absurdities of managed diversity caused more problems than they resolved, and that not all opposition to them could be dismissed as racist. Irving Levine, a seasoned intergroup relations expert who worked for Jewish organizations during the 1950s and '60s, told me years ago that "ethnotherapy" workshops uncover participants' "extraordinary ambivalence about their identity. Ethnicity is as explosive as sex, death, and money. . . . Ten different explosions can be waiting to happen in a room." Happen they do, as the political philosopher Jean Bethke Elshtain told me recently:

I mean, here are all these diversity trainers running around earning a living keeping people divided. The last thing they want is for other people to be anything but divided and suspicious. Otherwise, the trainers would be out of work. They treat people like infants, like jerks. They make it morally acceptable for some people to beat up on others because they were born a certain sex or gender. What do they invite? Only more hostility.

Confronted with this truth, the *Times* and other large corporations are adjusting their policies. When Sulzberger was crusading openly for liberal racism at the paper in 1994, he said:

> The culture change has to start with senior management. . . . [But] if the rest of the organization is going to wait for 100 percent of senior management to do 100 percent of diversity, we're never going to get anywhere. And middle managers and all the other employees have to commit to this just as strongly, because some senior managers aren't going to change until the pressure from the bottom is as strong as the pressure from the top. . . . Increasingly, any middle or senior manager's or any employee's advancement is going to depend on how he or she deals with these fundamental issues.

On December 1, 1996, a *Times* Week in Review section story by Claudia Deutsch on a "diversity" controversy at Texaco noted:

> Now some companies have added pragmatism to idealism. . . . Besides sending managers to diversity training they are telling them to change their behavior: either you help promote minorities and women with their careers, they are told, or your paycheck, and maybe your job, will be in jeopardy. . . . Of course, there are chief executives who believe that bigotry can be trained out of existence. It is often the people in the trenches, the ones who have tried that route, who say it is futile.
> . . . Edward N. Gadsden, a black man who became Texaco's director of diversity three years ago, puts much more stock in a new program to base part of managerial bonuses on the retention of minorities and women. "I am not in the business of attitudinal

change," he said. "We need to establish a culture that specifies the behaviors you will exhibit."

Champions of managed diversity seem to have forgotten, or never to have known, that there is an alternative to either heightening "awareness" of presumed cultural differences or, failing that, to parceling out rewards along color-coded lines, as Texaco seems to be doing. The better alternative is to nurture and reward people who can implement Thurgood Marshall's observation, "We will only attain freedom if we learn to appreciate what is different and muster the courage to discover what is fundamentally the same." Sulzberger wants employees to muster the courage to discover what is different. What does he fear might happen if they believed that, in most matters that count in public life, everyone is fundamentally the same?

◆ Racist Diversity

What Sulzberger fears but will not say, I think, is that if every manager adhered faithfully to classical liberal procedures and to standards scrubbed free of racial bias, fewer blacks would make the grade. Yes, there are many fine black journalists in American newsrooms, and, yes, sometimes a low estimation of blacks' readiness to compete is prompted by racism. But sometimes it's prompted by hard evidence which seasoned managers wish they had never seen but can no longer deny. For every story a black reporter tells about the "glass ceiling" that blocks black promotions, a white colleague can tell a story about "going the extra mile" for a young black reporter with substantial skill deficiencies and even, perhaps, a head full of demons that scrambled others' signals.

The point at which "different folkways" become "deficiencies" is a matter of dispute and confusion, of course. But there is nothing racist about acknowledging skill deficiencies— some of which may, indeed, reflect the legacies of racism that also become easier to acknowledge in a climate of candor about racism's costs. In *When Work Disappears*, the sociologist William Julius Wilson surveys urban employers, black as well as white, who are reluctant to hire young black men. These men described by the employers are culturally different, but is theirs a "difference" which anyone with work to do can respect? A shipping company or food-processing plant hasn't time or resources to cut damaged people much slack, least of all by characterizing their deficiencies as cultural differences.

At Harvard University or the *Times*, matters look different. Work at these institutions demands an extraordinary repertoire of skills, but they have their pick of the most talented black students, teachers, or journalists. If few blacks are hired or promoted, either racism in these institutions is worse than it is in businesses studied by Wilson, or there aren't enough blacks who've overcome racism's educational and emotional damage sufficiently to succeed. Both conclusions are troubling. And both are compatible: There can be both racism in a company *and* a terribly small pool of well-qualified black applicants. Yet the *Times* and most other upscale institutions lean toward the first assumption, which impels them to treat most disparities in black employees' performance as "cultural" differences.

That is a dangerous thing to do. In his *Two Nations*, Andrew Hacker, thinking to expose white prejudice against legitimate cultural "difference," writes that "unless blacks are willing to deny large parts of their selves," they are unlikely to succeed in "white" institutions such as airlines or university physics departments, where people "are expected to think and act in white ways." More respect should be given, he argues, to the fact that black culture is more "earthy" and less "linear" than white. Thus does liberal "diversity" become racism. If there were more candor about real deficiencies—measured not by standardized tests but by assessments of on-the-job performance by managers committed to "diversity"—there might be greater pressure from enlightened corporations like the *Times* and from national business councils for a concerted effort to enrich blacks' early educational experiences.

The less candor, on the other hand, the more likely a corporation will take refuge in unacknowledged double standards—or, when these fail, resort to rationalizations like Hacker's or like Rutgers University president Francis Lawrence's liberal "Freudian slip" about blacks' allegedly "genetic hereditary background"—a comment he made in 1994 during a feverish defense of campus double standards that had the effect of turning every black student into a walking placard for disadvantage. That is as racist as policies endorsed by Arthur Sulzberger, William Kunstler, or Andrew Hacker. Imagine running an institution that has separate admissions standards (though it denies it) for blacks and whites and that coddles disproportionate numbers of blacks with separate orientation sessions, shallow racial caucuses, and decorously second-rate evaluations. Even liberals who set up such systems soon find themselves assuming things about the intended beneficiaries which they never mention—except in a "slip" like Lawrence's. The result is precisely what liberals claim to find in others' racism: that it is all the more damaging for being unconscious. Now we know how they know.

Liberal racism of this sort leaves blacks in an excruciating bind. On the one hand, they can accept the condescension of liberals who, for political, moral, or ideological reasons, won't pay them the compliment of holding them to universal standards of achievement. (Some multiculturalists cop out by pretending that there *aren't* any universal standards.) On the other hand, blacks can assume that the only alternative to the unwitting disdain of a Francis Lawrence is the witting disdain of a Jesse Helms. In that case, they'll settle for Lawrence and defend his race-specific programs, as long as he'll promise never again to say what the programs imply. In their different ways, blacks and white liberals who accept this sad bargain hope to gain blacks enough mileage to offset disadvantages and insecurities. Yet racial corralling ill equips the most disadvantaged of blacks for success in market-driven venues. No wonder Lawrence's "slip" caused such embarrassment and pain.

One alternative to such debacles in education is the scholarly "boot camp" run by the historically black Roman Catholic Xavier College in Louisiana. As described by Ellis Cose, the Xavier program is rigorous and unrelenting in every way that most Rutgers programs for black students are not. A high proportion of Xavier graduates go on to good medical and other professional schools. They can do so because their mentors said to them what white liberals seem unable to say in institutions bent on "diversity" for its own sake: "Come on, we know you can achieve this! Stop grousing, work *much* harder, and we'll be there for you every step of the way."

Another alternative is the one which liberals claim would decimate black populations on campuses and in professional workplaces: Hold everyone rigorously to the same performance standards. That needn't mean dropping the black proportion of some student bodies from, say, 10 percent to 2. In 1995, when it seemed likely that California voters would defy liberal racism and pass a proposition to abolish affirmative action in state government (as they did 1996), the University of California organized rigorous precollege courses and training programs for thousands of black and Hispanic youths. The best of the programs are now applauded by whites, whose support is tempered only by wonderment that it took a "conservative" assault on racial double standards to prompt them.

Translating the applause into serious support will require less political vision and hard work than racist liberals think but more, apparently, than they themselves are ready to give. At the very mention of a possibility of a short-run drop in the proportion of black students at Berkeley or Rutgers, too many liberals stop thinking precisely where they should begin. If one pedagogical purpose of "diversity" is to break down commonly held stereotypes of people who are "different," why shouldn't an educational institution ensure that any black student its white students encounter is fully as qualified as they? Wouldn't that banish every excuse for stigma and give young whites more experiences with blacks who are truly their equals? When that principle is violated in the name of "diversity," students separate racially and barely communicate.

And if Sulzberger and other publishers are truly as

committed to black opportunity as they say, why don't they set up the journalistic equivalent of an Xavier College for young black reporters who need extra seasoning and discipline? Genetic racial deficiencies do not exist. Racist damage does exist. Yet rather than face it and deal with it at some short-run cost to their pocketbooks and their pretensions, liberals, no less than conservatives, keep slipping into the half-conscious, unfounded assumption of congenital inadequacy when they deny the realities before them—realities which the media, ironically, are supposed to report "without fear or favor."

When even an organization as hell-bent on achieving diversity as the *Times* find itself hitting a wall in minority hiring, it is time to realize that while all employers can and must stop perpetrating racist damage, few can *repair* damage already done. Neither a factory nor a college can turn itself into a remediation center; nor can a newspaper become a therapy group. Nor does it help matters to complain that distinguished institutions harbor mediocre whites, too, for, if that's true, and if those institutions aren't complacent about the racism, patronage, nepotism, or corruption that may have created the problem, then this is a new problem for management, not a solution for blacks who need more and deeper training.

Yet the mind-set that blocks candor extends not just to hiring but to news coverage and commentary—as Sulzberger insists it must. Let us explore a bit more closely that problem's origins in racial guilt.

◆ A Proud Racial Penitent

In 1993, Sulzberger, devoted to the rigors of managed diversity, gave command of the editorial page to Howell Raines, then fifty, a racially penitent white Southerner whose literary roots go back to a segregationist mind-set he has tried hard to leave behind. The black religion scholar C. Eric Lincoln, like Raines a native of Alabama, wrote recently that he first understood "the limitations of the journalistic enterprise as a reliable index of . . . our racial dilemma" in 1941, while reading W. J. Cash's newly published *The Mind of the South*, which nicely anticipates some of Raines's preoccupations with unmasking racist ideas for the enlightenment of Northern as well as Southern readers. Cash, himself a journalist, had migrated from South Carolina to Chicago, and, according to Lincoln, "his clever revelations caused a substantial ripple of excitement and titillation among the circles of northern and eastern literati who were always on the alert for a new Thomas Wolfe, or a William Faulkner . . . to rise up out of the South to entertain them with the charming drollery of that region. 'Penetrating and persuasive,' wrote the *New York Times* of *The Mind of the South*."

In Cash's often sardonic account, Southern whites kept blacks "out of mind" altogether, reducing them to "singing sad songs in the cotton" except when they affected to reward them by addressing them as Uncle Tom or " 'A'nt Mattie' with the peculiar affection and respect quality white folks reserve for their favorite black retainers," as Lincoln put it. Such solicitude, at once heartfelt and hypocritical, eased the consciences of elites who were keeping blacks down by turning poor whites against them. Gestures of affection served to displace elites' racism—and blacks' own resentment of it—onto "po' white trash," who, under such pressure from above and below, proceeded to richly deserve the contempt in which they were held. "[B]ehind the so-called rednecks who so readily laid down their bibles . . . to go 'coon huntin' was all the time the stealthy hand of the 'quality white folk' who taught the blacks to hate the 'white trash' in the first place," Lincoln recalls. "Mr. Cash calls these 'the best people,' and it was not until he laid bare the controlling mind of the South . . . that the vision of quality so carefully nurtured in the big house and its derivative institutions began to fade and drip."

Fifty years after Cash caused a ripple of excitement in Chicago and New York, Raines, then the *Times*'s Washington bureau chief, wrote a long, sentimental article in the newspaper's Sunday magazine about the hard life and high dignity of his own affluent family's canny black housekeeper, who had opened a pampered young white boy's eyes to a segregated world he couldn't otherwise have recognized as the soul-eating "jungle" it was. *Times* editors found "Grady's Gift" penetrating and persuasive enough to pull some strings to win a Pulitzer Prize for what snickering black reporters dubbed "Howell's mammy story." Like Cash's "best people," Raines seemed to sentimentalize blacks and, in other writing, to displace onto "white trash" a more explicit condescension, laced with contempt.

Whatever Grady taught young Raines, it did not propel him down from the campus of Birmingham-Southern University, where he was a student in the early 1960s, to join civil rights marchers in the city streets below. But later he did collect their reminiscences of the struggle in *My Soul Is Rested*, a nicely arranged oral history of the movement's glory years. "It was my way of saying I didn't have the courage to walk with Dr. King in 1963, but I plan to walk with him the rest of my life. That book represents a public declaration," Raines told *Atlanta Journal-Constitution* writer Don O'Briant thirty years later, when such public declarations brought honors, not risks. Rising through the ranks of *Times* correspondents, Raines wrote about racism in Johannesburg and London. He wrote about how elites in his and C. Eric Lincoln's native Alabama still used racism to mire the state in quasi-colonial subservience to distant corporate landholders.

Raines deserves respect for acknowledging the racism in his own roots; would that we were all as searching and candid about matters so close to home. Creditably, he turns his accounts of Southern life against Alabama's failed populism, rotten public finance, prison chain gangs, and tribal football rivalries. If he overpraises voting rights activists and can't see how others in the civil rights establishment have gone wrong, that is because he knows what the best of them endured while fighting real injustices. They had to steel themselves against whites' syrupy professions of color blindness and train themselves to attack the oppression smoldering behind facades of goodwill.

In an interview in *My Soul Is Rested*, the journalist Eugene

Patterson tells Raines how the legendary Ralph McGill, editor of the *Atlanta Constitution* in the 1950s, at first tried gently to help Southern elites comprehend that segregation had to go, only to conclude that "sometimes you have to come right out and punch a guy in the nose." Raines does a lot of punching, too, but sometimes he hits the wrong "guys," as in his attacks on all who criticize racial districting. "Every Southerner must choose between two psychic roads, the road of racism or the road of brotherhood," he has written. Such moral certitude, the *New Yorker*'s Peter Boyer observed, "can come across to other Southerners, even some 'good' ones, as wearisome piety."

It strikes good Northerners that way, too, especially when Raines tackles racial disputes that aren't best viewed through the lenses he carries with him. McGill was immersed self-effacingly in the life of a region he loved, and before he started "punching" anyone, he had to wrestle with his own long attachments to a segregated society. In contrast, Raines left the South and, the moment he got to the *Times* editorial page, came out punching. Clinton's federal crime bill "deserves to die," he wrote in 1994, because it excluded a proposed Racial Justice Act. Never mind that most of the Congressional Black Caucus voted for the crime bill without that act; Raines would keep their consciences. Patronizing blacks was part of the package: In Brooklyn, the long, ugly, often violent "boycott" of two Korean-owned stores by histrionic, hate-filled militants became, in a *Times* editorial, a demonstration by "a black neighborhood," which it certainly was not.

Liberals' obligation now is not just to expose and censure racism but to discredit the "diversity" mongering that gives racism a new lease on life. Today's Ralph McGill will need both the sympathy and the guts to show the civil rights establishment and chief executive officers that "managed diversity," like racial districting and the color-coding of criminal justice, bungles the pursuit of true integration and democracy. To say so isn't to roll back the clock to the days of all-white newsrooms and Jim Crow government; it is to acknowledge the irony in the spectacle of a few powerful white men, like Sulz-berger and Raines, directing people of all colors toward diversity, inside and outside the *Times*.

◆ A Comeuppance

Raines's moralism and Sulzberger's manic "diversity" mind-set reached something of a climax in the *Times*'s coverage and commentary during New York City's 1993 mayoral race. The paper reversed almost every truth about the former U.S. Attorney Rudolph Giuliani's winning campaign against David Dinkins, the city's first black mayor. The *Times*'s disdain for ordinary New Yorkers' resentment of Dinkins's record (much of that resentment felt by nonwhites) reached so high and shrill a pitch that it prompted unprecedented criticism in journalism reviews and other venues.

There was no good reason to think of Dinkins as any more successful a mayor than Abraham Beame, the city's first Jewish one, who had been turned out after one term. But the *Times*'s racial mind-set would not be denied. A Giuliani victory would fail to keep the city's "politics in line with its demographics. . . . In a profound sense, this son of the 1950s is running against history" read an important *Times* profile (July 25, 1993) of the candidate during the election. "Even if he wins, he may be the last white man for years to lead this city."

It was also accepted wisdom at the *Times* that Giuliani would "play the race card," stoking racist fears. Giuliani, understanding that a majority of the electorate consisted of blacks, Hispanics, Asians, and white liberals, made strenuous efforts to present himself as the apostle of racial inclusion. "If I could make up the two points I lost by in 1989 with only black votes, it'd be healthier for me and the city," he told me at the start of the 1993 campaign. Yet *Times* news coverage cast him relentlessly as the candidate of a white-ethnic restoration. When Giuliani called the election a referendum on Dinkins's competence, a *Times* reporter wrote that he was trying to "give voters a race-free excuse for voting against Mr. Dinkins."

When he protested the Dinkins camp's characterizations of him as a "fascist" and "racist," Raines found the protest reminiscent of "the heyday of [former Republican political guru] Lee Atwater"—never mentioning that Reagan administration veterans William Bennett and Edwin Meese had disowned Giuliani as "too liberal" and that Meese had endorsed his Conservative Party opponent.

When Giuliani won, the *Times* lost, not because the paper had endorsed Dinkins as much as because its coverage and commentary had distorted the city. Democracy is diminished when people with authority, especially the moral authority of a great newspaper, proclaim that racial differences, which they can barely define, are and should be "significant" in public and corporate life. To insist that such differences govern "how we see each other and how we see the news" is to encourage vulnerable people of all colors to view one another through ever-narrowing eyes. It is to let down those who are trying to keep faith with something American in everyone they meet.

News coverage and commentary should avoid encouraging readers and viewers to think of their fellow citizens, whatever their colors or surnames, as tiles in a "gorgeous mosaic." A mosaic never changes shape, size, or composition. If each of us is a tile in a fixed pattern, who or what is the bonding agent that holds society together? The paper's publisher? The marketing director? The U.S. assistant attorney general for civil rights? The question diversity trainers seldom pose is, How can *all* of us be trained to give part of ourselves to the social glue that binds us across differences of color in public meetings, workplaces, and on the street?

Since America really isn't a mosaic but an organism whose composition keeps changing, we might pose the question this way: Who or what will help to channel the country's protean energies away from Balkanization and dissolution and toward a better civic culture? If public policy and the media only heighten people's awareness of one another's religious and ethnic identities, they will hinder individuals' passages (and promotions) to a second, broader tier of American creativity and belonging. We need that second tier more than ever before. Precisely because the country is becoming more racially and religiously diverse, we should be working overtime to identify and nurture the *shared* values and affectional bonds that have spared it the fate of so many nations.

Yet too many who do work at this every day are unnoticed or disdained in the media. The *Times* ignored or stereotyped the men of all colors at the Promise Keepers rally at Shea; the worshippers of all colors at the pope's masses in New York and New Jersey; the white Southern voters who cast their ballots for black candidates in the 1996 elections; and the many thousands of Giuliani voters, including white liberals, Asians, and Hispanics, who realized that "rainbow" politics had failed them. Liberals may believe that color-coding our public life liberates the oppressed, but it is the freedom to cross racial and tribal lines that draws to America millions of people in flight from their homelands' traditional cobwebs and feuds. They don't want the patronizing, cookie-cutter designations that frame "diversity"-oriented coverage and commentary on racial districting, elections, school curricula, and religious rallies. Even American blacks, here longer than most of us and angered by media neglect or stereotyping, often resent corrective efforts to anoint everyone with a black skin the bearer of an "authentic" racial culture that exists only in reaction to the long-discredited American practice of coding by color.

We know how destructive such racial designations have been, here and around the world; what do we suppose would be the consequences of their becoming even more deeply ingrained in our public and corporate life? To its credit, the *Times* reported at length in 1996 that many "multiracial" couples and their offspring refuse to check any U.S. Census–designated ethnicities except "Other." They, too, are fleeing the scripted solidarities of the past. The media should stop reinforcing race loyalties. Journalists should take better account of the vigorous American irreverence that so often confounds racial and ethnic designations and loyalties—on playing fields, in cultural arenas, and especially in politics.

Of course, that American irreverence is not going to prevail in every public controversy or political campaign. But isn't it a great newspaper's mission to keep that hope alive, whether in congressional districts in Georgia and Florida or in the boroughs of the City of New York? Isn't it a great newspaper's mission to stand against racialism and help the American spirit soar?

Mightn't that even be good for a great newspaper's bottom line?

CHAPTER 5

WAY OUT OF AFRICA

◆ The Whiteness of Blackness

Even as Americans' notions of race become more fluid and ecumenical, the old idea that one's skin color determines one's destiny—and that it *should*—seems to be regaining ground among blacks. That isn't the fault only of diversity liberals in the media, Afrocentric writers and educators in schools, or race hustlers in politics and in the streets. Their doings are symptoms and, sometimes, accelerants of a more mysterious condition: a deepening uncertainty about the meaning of black identity in the United States—and, for that matter, anywhere else.

Sensationalized or not, the signs of confusion are proliferating. In recent years, prominent black leaders and activists have careened from precipitating a near breakdown of the NAACP to cheering black jury nullifications in cases like O. J. Simpson's; from flirting with Ebonics and dreaming of lost African glory to commercializing the celebration of Kwanzaa; from admiring Louis Farrakhan's pseudo-Islamic demagoguery to supporting the racial districting that has isolated black political leaders; from discouraging interracial marriages and adoptions to displaying a marked coolness toward the prospect of Colin Powell's running for president.

Black ambivalence about the larger society is hardly new. Ever since the abolitionist Frederick Douglass stunned a white Fourth of July audience in 1852 by asking, "What have I, or those I represent, to do with your national independence?" American blacks have been shadow-boxing with an all-enveloping whiteness, by turns both threatening and seductive. "Lure and loathing," the black scholar Gerald Early calls that ambivalence in the title of an anthology of essays by black writers addressing the problem. Black responses to whiteness oscillate between "fight" and "flight," between integrationism and separatism. "Can I be both [an American and a Negro]?" asked educator and writer W.E.B. Du Bois at the turn of the century. "Or is it my duty to cease to be a Negro as soon as possible and to become an American?"

By midcentury, black writers and leaders seemed to prefer the second option. But now the tension between calls to race loyalty and calls to transracial dignity is taking a new twist: The wide national acceptance of black celebrities, artists, professionals, intellectuals, and politicians—not to mention the loosening of the old Anglo-Saxon norms by other nonwhites and by "Anglos" themselves—has prompted new, complicated reflections. Even as some black Americans "pass" into an integration their forebears could barely have imagined, others' definitions of racism have become more exceptional, elusive, extenuated, and, paradoxically, more insistent. The conviction that racism is growing draws strength from incidents that are ballyhooed in the media and from new literary portraits and studies of black pain. Yet that conviction is shaken repeatedly by rising rates of white "crossover" voting, interracial marriage, the increase in earnings of two-income black families relative to those of white families, and other good news which liberals now ritually deny. Racism persists, but it cannot be the main source of confusion.

Why, then, does it seem so long since that Saturday night three decades ago when the Smothers Brothers crooned "The Lord Is Colorblind" to what CBS-TV must have assumed was a reasonably receptive national audience? Why would many blacks and white liberals now consider such a receptive audience naive, hypocritical, and even racist? Why do so many consider an assertion that color isn't important an insult to black pride?

For a moment in the mid-1970s, *Roots*, Alex Haley's saga of Africans' abduction into slavery here, seemed to have found an answer. Turning on an intrepid black writer's report of an astonishing encounter with his ancestral African past, it promised to weave a recovered black story into the American national myth whose promise, whatever it was, would become more coherent for resolving the ambiguities in its black story line. The story of *Roots's* rapid rise and descent sheds some light on the new ambiguity of black identity in an America whose own identity is increasingly ambiguous, too.

Published late in 1976, *Roots* became the next year's top nonfiction bestseller after a record 130 million Americans saw the twelve-hour television miniseries it inspired. At least 250 colleges began offering credit courses based significantly on *Roots*. Travel agencies packaged Back-to-Africa "Roots" tours. Even before television had anointed him white America's best-known interpreter of black experience since Martin Luther King, Jr., I watched Haley tell a rapt Harvard undergraduate audience, most of it black, about his breathtaking encounter with the *griot,* or oral historian, of a village in Gambia from which, Haley said, his ancestor Kunta Kinte had been abducted to America in 1767. When he noted, as he had in the book, that the *griot* had "had no way in the world to know that [his ancient African-village narrative] had just echoed what I had heard all through my boyhood years on my grandma's front porch in Henning, Tennessee," there were gasps, and then the packed Quincy House dining hall was awash in tears.

With this unprecedented return by a black American to the scene of the primal crime against his West African forebears— "an astonishing feat of genealogical detective work," Doubleday's original dust jacket called the book—a long, tortuous arc of dispossession and yearning for a historic reckoning seemed, at last, to come home. *Roots* wasn't just Haley's own story, it was "a symbolic history of a people," he told a British reporter who had raised doubts about its accuracy. "I, we, need a place called Eden. My people need a Pilgrim's Rock." What the black nationalist writer Harold Cruse called the "sleepless nightmare of nonrecognition" endured by millions of blacks like Haley's grandmother might be relieved, if not dispelled, by a glimpse of Kinte's fortitude in a brutal, bottomless absurdity.

That absurdity hadn't abated with emancipation. Even as some whites preached a "melting pot" Americanism that would transcend racial divisions, they provided for themselves along carefully patrolled racial lines. Such hypocrisy forced blacks to play a similar double-game—a dance, really—that alternated between deference and defiance, with many other steps in between. Sudden lurches toward integration in the 1960s threw these deft coping strategies into stark relief, scrambling the coordinates of an uneasy racial coexistence and confounding pious hopes for a smooth transition. Some white-ethnic Roman Catholics and Jews, regretting their own subordination to Anglo-Saxon ideals, resisted the racial integration even more, intensifying their subcultural identities as "unmeltable ethnics."

Some blacks responded to this and to their own doubts about assimilation with a retaliatory black parochialism, assailing other blacks whom they deemed too accommodating and forcing even assimilationist whites to acknowledge their own hyphenated Americanism. Hollywood got into the act, spoofing Jewish assimilation in films like *Goodbye, Columbus*, and generating blaxploitation films, like *Putney Swope* and *Shaft*, that parodied integration. Suddenly it was unclear whether the nation would move toward a new synthesis or slip back into the racial and ethnic enclaves the melting pot's champions had hoped to dissolve.

Appearing amidst all this confusion, *Roots* at first startled, then relieved pessimists on both sides of the color line. By the grace of Haley's pilgrimage, it seemed, blacks would recover and share the true story of their dispossession, prying open some secrets of an American nightmare wisdom whites had barely known. At last, the country might weave its black threads into a fabric resilient enough to sustain a decorous pluralism of peoples and a decent integration of persons. Coming less than fifteen years after King's speech at the Lincoln Memorial, Haley's mythopoeic triumph tugged at people's hearts and certified a realignment in the national cosmos. Americans of all colors were transfixed by Haley's account, even as charges emerged—some in an early review by the historian Willie Lee Rose in the *New York Review of Books*—that *Roots* contained critical historical errors, unacknowledged fabrications, and an indeterminate amount of plagiarism from recent novels. Haley received a "special" Pulitzer Prize, an unprecedented "Citation of Merit" from a National Book Awards panel, and many other accolades and honorary degrees. Two years later, ABC-TV produced a second series, *Roots: The Next Generation*, based on Haley's new book *Search*, chronicling his family's later triumphs and tribulations, including Haley's work on *The Autobiography of Malcolm X*, which he said had inspired the search for his own forebears that took up the series's final episode. "Now, as before," wrote Frank Rich on February 19, 1979 (he was then at *Time* magazine), "*Roots* occupies a special place in the history of our mass culture; it has the singular power to reunite all Americans, black and white, with their separate and collective pasts."

Today, *Roots* is seldom mentioned. The History Channel's twentieth-anniversary broadcast of the original series in February 1997 was little remarked on by viewers or print commentators. The book is still in stores—a Doubleday spokesman says it remains "an important title on the Dell [paperback books] backlist"—but it's not much read in college or high school courses. "*Roots*?" laughs C. Eric Lincoln. "It's disappeared! Alex Haley was my friend, and I can tell you he was a journeyman freelance writer, not a political writer or historian. He was given a status that he didn't deserve or expect." The black press seldom mentions him, except in connection with Malcolm X's autobiography. Comedian Richard Pryor parodied *Roots* with a skit about a black American beseeching an African village *griot* to tell him about his ancestors. The *griot* hands him a photograph. "But, that's a *white* man," sputters the visitor. *"Tell me where I'm from."* The *griot* rummages through his materials and replies, "You're from *Cleveland,* nigger!" It is almost as if Haley's effort has been airbrushed or laughed out of history and popular culture.

Roots's virtual disappearance can't be rationalized by claiming that it accomplished its mission by transforming the consciousness of a generation. What will the next and later generations learn from today's Afrocentric stories, so many of which are less about blacks' introduction to America than about the glories of ancient Egypt? These stories did not displace *Roots*; they tried to fill a vacuum it had left unfilled. Nor is it enough to claim, as some of Haley's critics did, that *Roots* shortchanged women by portraying them as passive helpmates to men like Kunta Kinte; Haley's misconstruals have been more than redressed by Alice Walker, Toni Morrison, Maya Angelou, and many other black women, but few authors now offer strong, redemptive narratives to young black men.

Haley embarrassed his true believers by taking folklore and fictional liberties with a narrative he'd claimed was historically true. He fabricated "discoveries" about Kinte and even recycled others' fiction, settling out of court for $650,000 with author Harold Courlander, passages of whose novel *The Africans* he had pretty much copied. C. Eric Lincoln recalls that many members of the Black Academy of Arts and Letters considered *Roots* fraudulent in literary as well as historical terms because they viewed Haley as less than a true writer and the book itself as more cinematic than "interior" in the ways that written fiction can be. But, by that standard, a lot of popular "history," from Marco Polo's accounts of a Far East he may never have visited, to Parson Weems's fanciful portraits of George Washington, long in McGuffey's *Reader,* should have been retired sooner than they were.

While *Roots* was denounced as a scholarly "fraud" by the historian Oscar Handlin, it was defended as an irresistible historical novel and pedagogical tool by other historians such as Bernard Bailyn, Robert Fogel, Edmund S. Morgan, and David Brion Davis, who told the *New York Times,* "We all need certain myths about the past, and one must remember how much in the myths about the Pilgrims or the immigrants coming here has been reversed." Morgan called it "a statement of someone's search for an identity," noting that Paul Revere and his "midnight ride" were unknown until Longfellow wrote a poem about it. But the black writer James A. McPherson says of such rationalizations, "They were like the last whiff of a condescending liberalism, saying 'Let's give them at least *that!*' "

What drained *Roots* of its power with the public—black as well as white—was a loss of faith in the myth itself, a disillusionment in at least three dimensions.

First, Haley had dissembled a lot about Africa. He depicted a precolonial Eden that hadn't existed; created his account of Kunta Kinte's youth there more out of current anthropology than history; paired all that with the story of his own communing with village elders in *post*colonial Gambia; and wildly inflated black Americans' expectations of sub-Saharan Africa, past and present. Sudan, Ethiopia, Somalia, Rwanda, Burundi, Zaire—one could double the list before finding a sub-Saharan nation that isn't now run by thugs, wracked by bloody tribal wars, or watching hundreds of thousands starve. Black Americans visiting such places have experienced "solidarity" with their inhabitants only by letting skin color eclipse virtue and blaming everything on the legacies of colonialism. Africans can't do that because they are busy fighting other black Africans, as did their precolonial forebears, who enslaved and sold millions of people to the whites who transported them here. This is not hyperbole; it is a reality which it takes hyperbole to deny, especially now that South Africa no longer serves as a foil against which black nations to its north can be made to seem more grand, or at least legitimate, simply for being black.

In a second dimension, though, Haley wasn't just distorting history; he was juggling archetypes. "Just as he poured Malcolm [X's] life into a Western literary paradigm of suffering and redemption that would appeal to whites as well as blacks, he took a whole people and poured it into a paradigm that wasn't its own," says Gerald Early. Unlike classical, mythical accounts of the Hebrew slaves' exodus from Egypt and the Puritans' "errand into the wilderness" around Plymouth Rock, *Roots* wasn't a product of its protagonists' own mother culture. It was the work of a deeply Western, Christian, American writer who took as much from Hebrews and Puritans as from Africans. Gerald Early thinks Haley may have taken a little, too, from the Southern myth of the noble lost cause, evoked so powerfully in Margaret Mitchell's *Gone With the Wind*. If there was any nobility in Haley's attempt to weave blacks more smoothly and clearly into the American tapestry—to make Kunta Kinte a mythic *American* figure like Paul Revere—there was also something historically tragic, though potentially redemptive, in the fact that he had to use the abductors' language and metaphysical looms.

That hard truth is irreversible, and we need to comprehend it, for the hope that Haley's impulse can be redeemed may be America's best hope. In a nation born of fraught departures, clean breaks, and fresh starts on new frontiers, the special difficulties that attach to explaining how blacks came here and what they lost along the way make them more critical to our shared destiny than is any other minority. Dragged here, not lured, they "had to construct their moral universe almost out of nothing, almost heroically, in the cauldron of slavery," says the black economist and social critic Glenn Loury:

> Becoming Christians kept them afloat and gave them strength to deal with a tremendously oppressive situation; the [black writer] Albert Murray says we are "the omni-Americans," people whose faith in this country rose highest because the alternative was total despair. As my friend Nathan Huggins put it, "We're not an alien population; we're *the alienated* population." We're after getting our birthright. We're the son who hasn't been acknowledged. See, *that binds you.* You can't turn back from it. Part of what I want is an acknowledgment of my place, my legitimacy, my belonging. (Interview with author)

The special depth of this need to end the sleepless nightmare of nonrecognition is what makes blacks "America's metaphor," as Richard Wright called them—America's best cultural barometers and moral witnesses, as well as its harshest, sometimes nihilist, assailants. Not to understand this—and liberals and conservatives both have their distinctively willful ways of misunderstanding it—is not to know one's country. We should try harder. Haley was trying to help.

Finally, though, *Roots* failed to take hold not only because Haley had to dissemble and juggle what myths he had about Africa, but because the myths themselves are losing their coherence to a newly implacable mass-marketing of novelty and instant gratification that deepens collective amnesia. "Increasingly we are learning that an individual's moral character is formed by narrative and culture," writes the sociologist Alan Wolfe. "Contracts between us are not enforced by laws or economic incentives; people adhere to social contracts when they feel that behind the contract lies a credible story of who they are and why their fates are linked to those of others." If neither laws nor material prosperity can substitute for a credible account of black identity, that is partly because America no longer has a credible account of its own.

We have always been reckless about this, and, like golf superstar Tiger Woods, millions of Americans have no single racial, ethnic, or religious identity that is rooted in a communal narrative. Whether anything creative or exalted can come of our life together along *this* new frontier is the American Question, and all power to those who engage it. But, at this point in our journey, it is time to say candidly that our national prospects are daunting, for we are losing not only the old communal subcultures but Western mythology's profoundly tragic sense of life. Because Haley tried to skirt the latter by telling an upbeat story for the mass market, *Roots* became our latest "Myth for a Day," turning immense historical pain into immense profit. That was what the slave trade had done, of course, and it was what *Roots* was meant to counter. But Haley's TV-friendly, docudramatic tale of black dispossession subtly reinforced the moral neutrality of classical liberalism, where markets are stronger than myths and history's tragic truths are not so much falsified as tamed.

Roots's acknowledgments lavishly credit Murray Fisher, an editor at *Playboy* magazine who helped Haley "structure this book," whose "story line . . . he then shepherded throughout. Finally," writes Haley, "in the book's pressurized completion phase, he even drafted some of *Roots*'s scenes. . . ."

One consequence of this bargain with mass marketing is the emergence of an *ersatz* tribalism, the sort of race-loyal posturing that was exposed, ironically, in a young black man's shouting "Only in America!" as he exulted outside the Los Angeles County courthouse over the Simpson criminal trial aquittal. *Ersatz* tribalism, oriented as much to the media as to the spirit, has been evident, as well, in the rise of Louis Farrakhan, who claims that he was taken by aliens into outer space—which sounds, ironically, rather like what Kunta Kinte must really have felt what was happening to him. Such responses seem a lot more facile and self-indulgent than the truly heroic struggles which Haley meant to evoke by turning Kunta Kinte into a composite of Nat Turner and Sojourner Truth.

If there was any saving grace in Haley's Faustian bargain, it was that, as mass entertainment, *Roots*'s did make blacks seem more "American" to whites who hadn't acknowledged how deeply American they are. However ephemeral, *Roots*'s success also showed Americans of all colors that blacks' destiny is here, not in Africa. For all the Nation of Islam's proclamations to the contrary, even Farrakhan knows this, at least in the half of his deeply troubled mind that isn't in Sudan praising African slavers. Not for nothing did he hold his march on the Washington Mall, surrounded by all those white monuments, rather than in Chicago's South Side, or in the part of the Mississippi Delta that his predecessor Elijah Muhammad's enthusiasts and other activists designated as the provisional seat of the Republic of New Africa in late 1960s. Had he done that, a lot fewer black men would have come. In Washington, Loury recalls being moved by the sight of many black men regarding those monuments as their own. But how enduring is that sense of belonging? The story of *Roots*'s own demise deepens the question but only partially answers it.

◆ Africa: There Is No "There" There

On the bright side, at least from an American civic cultural perspective, the *Roots* myth foundered first on disillusionment with a Pan-African vision—but also with "blackness" itself. In a dozen books and countless speeches and conversations, American blacks who made pilgrimages inspired by Haley's epiphanies reported the perplexing discovery (often painful, sometimes relieving) that they have no common destiny with Africa, in part because they share very little across the hundreds of tribal and linguistic lines that keep even Africans from having any common history with one another beyond that imposed by Europe.

Once the visitors got past their often European- or American-trained African hosts, they found what Eddy L. Harris described in 1992 in *Native Stranger: A Black American's journey into the heart of Africa*, and what *Washington Post* correspondent Keith Richburg recounted in a grieving, confessional essay in 1995 (later expanded into a book, *Out of America*): bitter disillusionment in encountering a continent they had hoped, even expected, to love. American Afrocentrists and liberal whites who sought a romantic, Pan-African foil to whatever they loathed in America found that millions of Africans are no more compatible with one another than are Croatians, Serbians, and Bosnians even now—all of them Slavic, as well as white, yet many of them guilty of "ethnic cleansing."

Similarly, while black American pilgrims to Africa were newly preoccupied with the significance of being "black," they found that that designation has no significance in most of Africa. There, the same skin color encompasses multitudes of cultural and tribal differences and is no more useful a moral or political lens than is "white" in the Balkans or, for that matter, in Scandinavia. Many Africans, recognizing their black visitors immediately as Americans, treated them as aliens having nothing in common with Africans who hadn't studied here or followed American culture. When the Reverend Johnny Ray Youngblood of Brooklyn made his first "Roots" trip to Ghana in 1990—prompted by a congregant's discovery of his own ties there—he identified himself as "African American" on a customs form. A Ghanaian official crossed out "African," saying, firmly, "You are *American*."

Other Africans mistook visiting black Americans at first glance for natives, whereupon they treated them as tribal enemies or as allies, depending solely on each individual's "ethnic" looks. When the *Washington Post*'s Richburg was entering Zaire, the customs official eyed him and insisted, despite Richburg's denials, that he was really a Zairian with a phony American passport. "Finally, I thought of one thing to convince him," Richburg writes. " 'Okay,' I said, pushing my French to its limit, 'suppose I was a Zairian. And suppose I did manage to get myself a fake American passport. . . . Tell me, why on Earth would I be trying to sneak back into Zaire?' The immigration officer pondered this for a moment, churning over in his mind the dizzying array of possibilities a fake U.S. passport might offer. . . . 'You are right,' he concluded, as he picked up his rubber stamp and pounded in my entry. 'You are American. . . .' " In Somalia, a gunman guarding a militia leader raced up to Richburg, shoved him to the ground, and took aim. One of the strongman's assistants rescued him and apologized, explaining, "You look like a Somali. He thought you were someone else."

In more historical terms, "the tie to Africa is an empty hope for Americans. All there is is remnants and echoes," says Glenn Loury, who keeps in touch with former students teaching in several African nations. Black Americans' only coherent memories and myths begin in the holds of the slave ships to which other Africans consigned them—a point that haunted Maya Angelou on a visit to Ghana, as she found herself wondering whether some of her hosts' ancestors had helped to sell hers. "During the long history of the Atlantic slave trade," write the historians James M. McPherson, Gary Gerstle, et al., in *Liberty, Equality, Power*, "nearly every African shipped overseas had first been enslaved by other Africans." One couldn't learn that from *Roots*, where Haley has two white men kidnap Kunta Kinte. That is not how most African enslavement began.

Richburg's *Out of America*, which has prompted heated

discussions among black journalists and authors, describes how some visiting black Americans' historical amnesia and misplaced enthusiasms made him realize that he's not only more American than African, but more American than *African-*American. Recalling an "African-American Summit" in Gabon that brought "black American civil rights activists and business leaders together with African government officials and others," he laments that

> at a time of profound change across Africa—more and more African countries struggling to shed long-entrenched dictator-ships—not one of the American civil rights luminaries ever talked about "democracy" . . . or "political pluralism.". . . Instead, what came out was a nauseating outpouring of praise from black Ameri-cans for a coterie of some of Africa's most ruthless strongmen and dictators. There were such famous champions of civil rights as Jesse Jackson, heaping accolades on the likes of Nigeria's number one military thug at the time, Gen. Ibrahim Babangida. . . .
>
> I had seen that kind of display before around Africa: black Americans coming to the land of their ancestors with a kind of touchy-feely sentimentality straight out of *Roots*. The problem is, it flies smack into the face of a cold reality.
>
> Last March in the Sudanese capital of Khartoum, I ran into a large group of black Americans who were . . . being given VIP treatment by the Sudanese regime. . . . The U.S. ambassador in Khartoum had the group over to his house, and the next day, the government-controlled newspaper ran a front-page story on how the group berated the ambassador . . . [and told him] that it was unfair to label the Khartoum regime as a sponsor of terrorists and one of the world's most violent, repressive governments. After all, they said, they themselves had been granted nothing but cour-tesy, and they had found the dusty streets of the capital safer than most crime-ridden American cities.

"I was nearly shaking with rage," Richburg wrote. "I couldn't even bring myself to write 'African Americans' in this essay." This from a man who in 1967 had watched some black resi-dents of his native Detroit "burn a large part of the city to the ground." Even were Detroit as bad as Khartoum, it would be hard to understand a typical black Detroit resident preferring Khartoum, and equally hard to imagine a black American preferring to live in Africa.

An Afrocentrist might counter that surely whites would feel comfortable in other parts of Europe, especially England or France, which are historically important to American identity. That's true. And it must be why writers and artists like James Baldwin, Richard Wright, Paul Robeson, Chester Himes, Josephine Baker, Dexter Gordon, Claude McKay, and other black Americans felt more comfortable there than they would have in Africa. Even as they turned their backs on a racist America, some of them reflected insightfully on the discovery that they were irreversibly American—indeed, "Western." Attending a Pan-African conference in Paris in 1956, Baldwin noted, in his essay "Princes and Powers," that the strongest opponents of European colonialism depended on Western values and languages to make their case to their fellow Africans. Just as these writers preferred Paris to Accra or Lagos, thousands of middle-class *Africans* who could be helping to run their black nations have also chosen to live in Europe and America. Something more than race is in play here, something both good and bad: a larger human destiny which Western universalism has done much to illuminate, if little to resolve.

European colonization did forever change the continent some Africans are fleeing. It is difficult to exaggerate—yet curiously difficult for some blacks to acknowledge—how overwhelming and all-enveloping was the European presence, not for every African individual and society, but decisively for all of the African social structures and states that might have kept the invaders at bay had they been stronger and more unified. "Whatever Africans share," writes Kwame Anthony Appiah, the Ghanaian philosopher now at Harvard, "we do not have a common traditional culture, common languages, a common religious or conceptual vocabulary. . . . We do not even have a common race. . . . This is not to deny that there are strong living traditions of oral culture . . . in most of the 'traditional' languages of sub-Saharan Africa, or to ignore the importance of a few written traditional languages." But they were too diffused to mount an African alternative of the scale and power of the European presence.

Even the work of such celebrated Pan-African writers as Wole Soyinka and Chinua Achebe presupposes what Appiah calls "the recognition that a specifically African identity began as the product of a European gaze." They write and are read almost exclusively in English and French. When the Kenyan writer Ngugi wa Thiong'o chose to write in Gikuyu, his mother tongue, members of other Kenyan ethnic groups regarded him, wrongly, as a tribal partisan. Even some of the more local, apparently indigenous African traditions were actually concocted in response to, and sometimes with the tactical support of, the white colonizers, complained the anticolonialist, Parisian-educated African writer Frantz Fanon, whose *The Wretched of the Earth* was a bible for Third World liberation movements. To build those movements, Africans had to create "national" identities and liberations using European military, economic, philosophical, and linguistic tools. "In a sense," writes Appiah, reflecting on Ngugi's experience, "we have used Europe's languages because in the task of nation-building we could not afford politically to use each other's." In another sense, the African writers' explorations of the subtle, often nonracial ironies of oppression, resistance, and liberation depend on Western philosophical and literary resources.

Afrocentrists who object that the West owes many of its own conceptual and even technological powers to ancient African civilizations like Egypt never explain why those purported advances didn't penetrate sub-Saharan Africa beyond Nubia and Kush. Racial differences seem to correlate with cultural ones, but a glance at Europe's gypsies, medieval Russian serfs, and millions of illiterate, barely functional whites elsewhere in the world suggests other, historical contingencies. Whatever the truth, whites' own ghastly, bloody misadventures since 1914 remind us that the West's "strengths" often ratchet up human folly into unprecedented levels of barbarity. We are still far out of Eden, and even the notion, embraced by some Afrocentrists in a retaliatory way, that skin color carries a common destiny is itself the detritus of the bad scientific and cultural beliefs that bedraped nineteenth-century European imperialist states in all their clanking, blundering glory.

One lesson is that racial solidarity goes nowhere, even as a response to racial imperialism. No "racial" identity concocted that way can endure, especially in America. In *Plural But Equal*, Harold Cruse offers a cautionary example:

> It was once the custom of West Indians to flaunt the history of Haiti and its glorious revolution under Toussaint L'Ouverture. . . . The innuendo was that American blacks had never fought for their freedom. But the 1980s saw the unprecedented spectacle of Haitian refugees risking death by drowning in shark-infested seas to gain entry into the United States—the land of freedom, liberty, and opportunity—*in the racist southern state of Florida, no less!* . . . Yet, the most vociferous supporters of the rights of black Haitians to the privileges of American citizenship were American blacks! . . . If their black American citizenship is so empty and unrewarding, why . . . champion the rights of Third World peoples (especially black ones) to emigrate to the United States?

The black writer Albert Murray, a friend of the late Ralph Ellison, could have admonished the American black luminaries visiting Gabon and the Sudan with a comment he made in 1996. Noting that the Jeffersonian idea that all are equal didn't come from Africa, he remarked in a C-Span interview in 1996 that when "the captive Africans who came to consciousness in the United States . . . went off on the Underground Railroad . . . they were not trying to get back to the tribal life in Africa. . . . They have no birthrights anywhere in the world except in America."

◆ Says Who? The Problem of Myths

If it is difficult to exaggerate white colonialism's influence on the African continent, it is impossible to exaggerate its effects on the Africans it transported into utterly alien realms. In America, the remnants of African cultures could hardly prevail against the ascendant missionary, civic, and mercantile dispensation. It is here that an understanding of Haley's mythical constructions must begin. His resort to "Eden" and "Pilgrim's [Plymouth] Rock" metaphors to characterize his book (even if only to market and defend it) illuminates something he couldn't conceal yet couldn't quite admit: *Roots* is an expression not of African cultural traditions, which made little of the mass abductions, but of Western European religious, literary, and political canons that had no real counterparts in Kunta Kinte's precolonial home.

Haley's intent was to weave sub-Saharan Africa's diffuse cultural threads into a Western myth of "exile" or "pilgrimage" for a black American audience that had internalized such notions from the Old Testament and Christianity, and for other Americans who needed to understand, in both Christian and liberal-Enlightenment terms, what their own forebears had perpetrated or suborned. Only with those Western compasses could Haley's redemptive journey be undertaken. (For that matter, as the investigative reporter Mark Ottaway of the London *Times* discovered, Haley's *griot,* too, was a dubiously traditional, somewhat Westernized operator whom Gambian advisers had tipped off to what Haley was hoping to hear.)

But—even had Haley's *griot* been authentic; even had Haley not mischaracterized, as an African Eden, a village whose leaders had done a brisk business with white slave traders at his ancestors' expense; even had he not invented the circumstances of Kunta Kinte's departure and imputed to the ship's passengers snatches of dialogue copied from Harold Courlander's novel; and even if, as Haley and his defenders insisted, *Roots* isn't a work of historical scholarship but a myth no less valuable than that of Moses leading the Israelites out of Egypt or the Pilgrims celebrating the first Thanksgiving—there remained this more consequential problem: *Roots* represents an attempt to re-create, in a Judeo-Christian idiom, a journey which millions of Africans did *not* undertake like the Hebrew slaves heading for the Promised Land.

Because it is not the offspring of its black protagonists' own mother cultures, *Roots* prescribes for them a tragic but ultimately redemptive sojourn in a Western, biblical diaspora. Ultimately, *Roots* is a Western account of a monstrous Western crime—a crime only according to Western religious and political standards that triumphed later when the British Empire and other European regimes abolished slavery as no African authority had done and as some African ethnic groups in the Sudan and Ghana have yet to do now. It was those same Western standards that triumphed still later in the freedom-loving impulses of writers from W.E.B. Du Bois to Fanon.

If there is any glory for the West in all this, it lies not in Western power but in Western thought, which projects triumphs out of tragedies and which, for all its depredations, nourishes the capacity for rational self-contradiction that alone has put words like "democracy," "liberation," and "human rights" on lips around the globe. The West's true Eden is not Haley's bucolic African village but the home of a serpent and a corruptible couple of human beings. It was in distorting this Eden that Haley—like countless Western writers before him—shrank from the tragic Western truth about human dignity that began with the story of the Fall.

The emblematic fumbler of this contradiction was Du Bois, who spent his last years in Ghana because, carrying the nineteenth-century West's own racist and rationalist notions too far, he had talked himself into a Pan-African fantasy so rickety and irrational that he eventually had to buttress it with another unsustainable fantasy, world communism. He abjured a third, less coherent yet more promising option: the American one, which Americans themselves seem always about to destroy but somehow never quite do.

♦ Their "There" Is Here

Exposing Africa's dismal past and the inadequacies of Haley's myth does not suggest black inferiority, as some whites seem to believe. It is, rather, a necessary if hardly sufficient condition of blacks' *American* rise from an abyss of captivity so vast it made

Gertrude Stein say, "They were not suffering from persecution, they were suffering from nothingness."

"The concept of historic reparation grows out of man's need to impose a degree of justice on the world that simply does not exist," writes Shelby Steele in *The Content of Our Character*. "Suffering can be endured and overcome; it cannot be repaid." Ironically, unfairly, some of the most important solutions always lie with the victims. At some of the most critical moments of any struggle, only they have the power to overcome the oppressor's weapons and deceits.

Blacks who have made it out of their New World abyss have done so first by using the very tools with which it was created. Most of the black American writers who speak in these pages anticipated the challenge that now faces everyone: We are all being "abducted" from our ancient mythical wellsprings and moorings by forces we no longer control and do not fully comprehend. It is thanks significantly to blacks, who started from "nothingness" here, that America—itself unprecedented and self-inventing even when blacks arrived—has an even better head start on a now global problem. Europeans sometimes say, as the Swiss psychologist C. G. Jung did first, that white Americans walk and talk "black." That fits neatly with some Africans' feeling that black Americans are not "black" at all. Again, the designation is meaningless.

Yet neither the real America nor the one we envision—whether we are libertarians or socialists, strict constructionists or judicial activists—can fulfill its raceless destiny without the people whites called "Negroes," "blacks," and "African Americans" when whites were on their best, but still misguided, behavior. America needs blacks not because it needs blackness but because it needs what they've learned on their long way *out* of blackness—that which others can't learn on the journeys they need to take out of whiteness.

And what have blacks learned?

Stanley Crouch in *The All-American Skin Game*:

From the Old Testament's tragic vision of human frailty, from the Passion of Christ and perhaps the greatest blues line ever written,

"Father, why hast Thou forsaken me?" Negroes fashioned one side of their vision. [On the other side,] perhaps from the incantational percussion of Africa, and what I can only call a heroic recognition of the vibrance at the center of existence, Negroes have transmuted pathos and tragedy into exultation through the rhythmic lyricism of swing . . . a congress of form and human feeling. . . .

African kingdoms, real or invented, make no impression on how I see myself, primarily because Africa had absolutely nothing to do with the conception of the ideas that eventually led to the end of slavery and were so essential to the recent history in which people the world over became more and more involved in breaking down the reign of South African apartheid. The international recognition and support of Nelson Mandela were born of the evangelical humanism at the center of modern democracy, which has no precedents in anything of African origin. It was Negro Americans, not Africans, who were central to the enriching of that humanism through their role in the difficult evolution of American democracy.

Harold Cruse in *Plural But Equal*:

The history of America and the world since World War II, and especially since the emergence of Martin Luther King and the civil rights movement, amply demonstrates that out of the international turmoil of social revolutions, wars, atrocities . . . the United States, with all its flaws and imperfections, takes on the semblance of the "best of all possible worlds.". . . This is especially true, and ironically so, for American blacks, who are just about the only nonwhite minority group in the entire world having no options to pack up and emigrate anywhere (including the African continent). For better or worse, the American black minority is stuck with the American version of political and capitalistic democracy. . . . There will be no social revolutions in the United States because historically the American nation is an evolutionary society. . . .

Gerald Early in *Civilization* magazine:

Afrocentrism is a historiography of decline, like the mythic epic of the [lost, antebellum] South. The tragedy is that black people fail to see their "Americanization" as one of the greatest human triumphs of the past 500 years.

O. J. Simpson's cheerleaders were "un-American," one might retort. Yes, they were—like the countless cheerleaders for countless whites acquitted in mere simulacra of trials across blacks' long sleepless nightmare of nonrecognition. Farrakhan's support for African slavers today is "un-American" certainly—but much of this country was built by people who collaborated with such slavers. The oft-highlighted black "pathologies" are indeed incompatible with an American civil society that relies heavily on individual conscience, not colorized absolution or blame—a society whose genius is, again, as the American literary historian Daniel Aaron put it, to be "ethical and pragmatic, disciplined and free." But just as incompatible with such a society are the pathologies recorded on nineteenth-century police blotters and "vice" investigations concerning Irish-Americans in New York City's Hell's Kitchen, and in Henry Adams's despairing observations about the limited capacities of Jewish immigrants on the Lower East Side.

In a country that has lost its moral bearings and collective memory, indicting racism in order to excuse Simpson, Farrakhan, gangsta rappers, "crack mothers," and lethal kids only reinforces perceptions of immutable racial differences that are already disproven. We are all led downhill, too, by moral posturing on either side of the subtly color-coded ideological line behind which conservatives blame everything on black "pathology," while blacks (and white liberals) blame "angry white men."

Blacks who have thought most deeply and productively about this are shedding a defensive blackness to join with whites who disown both their own past supremacy and their counterproductive guilt. They would have us forget Alex Haley's Africa, except as citizens of the world. They would have us recover the tragic realism in Western myths and stop our ears against the racial siren songs that sometimes echo within those myths and, still, within ourselves. They would have us become Americans. Much as there is to learn from the old solidarities we are shedding, and many as are their treasured remnants and lessons, the time is approaching when Americans of all colors will have to give their racial banners decent burials and kiss even their hyphens goodbye. The question is whether we can renew or rebuild a civic culture worth joining and defending. The answer turns on whether we can discard both blackness and whiteness as we have known them.

CHAPTER 6

MANY COLORS, ONE CULTURE?

◆ A Look Beyond Race

If one looks at the most admirable efforts by activists to over-come racial oppression in the United States, what one finds are people who yearn for justice, not merely for the advancement of a particular group. One finds people who do not replicate the racial alienations of the larger society but instead welcome interracial intimacy of the most profound sorts. One finds people that are not content to accept the categories of communal affiliation that they inherit but instead insist upon bringing into being new and better forms of communal affiliation ... in which love and loyalty are unbounded by race.

—Law professor Randall Kennedy,
speaking at Columbia University,
1996

But, this is where the ambiguity enters. There is an elemental tension between the existential necessity of black self-development and the moral requirements of a humanism which transcends race. One draws on ties of blood, shared history and common faith. The other endeavors to achieve an integration of the most wretched, despised, and feared of our fellows along with the rest of us into a single political community of mutual concern. One takes the social fact of race as a given, even celebrating it. The other aims to move beyond race altogether.

—Glenn Loury,
in *Commonquest,*
a black/Jewish journal, Fall 1966

The first time I heard Randall Kennedy speak publicly on the subject of "Racial Pride, Racial Kinship, and Other Problems," many of his listeners seemed sullen, or, at best, subdued. Kennedy, a rising star in our dark night of racial legal contention, was delivering a rigorous attack on liberal racist thinking to more than a hundred mostly liberal academics and students, about half of them black, in Columbia University's 1996 Lionel Trilling Lecture. Eight months later, when I heard him give a shorter version of the same talk to eight hundred undergraduates in the political philosopher Michael Sandel's Justice course at Harvard, the response was more open-minded. The students' buoyant, if skeptical, engagement with his argument was even more impressive in light of the fact that he debated it first with Sandel, the "authority figure" in the room. Sandel was defending not liberal racism but the idea that we do have obligations to some groups to which we are bound by birth, history, or necessity, but not necessarily by choice.

At both Columbia and Harvard, Kennedy opened by asking, "What is the proper role of race in determining the way I, an American black, should feel toward others?" His answer, which he elaborated analytically and anecdotally for half an hour, was, "Neither race pride nor racial kinship offers guidance that is intellectually, morally, or politically acceptable." Clearly, he meant to push or carry color-blind humanism beyond what most blacks, and even most white liberals, today consider a racial breaking point. Insisting that any race is merely "a conglomeration of strangers," he cast a cold eye on even the apparent solidarity of the Million Man March, wondering aloud how most of the men who called one another "Brother" would have responded had someone asked, "Would you be willing to loan $100 to this brother? . . ."

Kennedy then deepened his attack "on assumptions which privilege . . . the loyalties of blood . . . over chosen loyalties, the loyalties of will." As he has in the media and as a participant in a high-profile lawsuit, he defended (white) foster parents' custody of (black) children against the claims of natural (black) parents who had abandoned them or had had them taken away after abusing them, but, years later, wanted them back. No blood tie could excuse violating the children's dignity and the foster parents' voluntary, "loving effort," he said. "In my view, many people, including legislators and judges, make far too much of blood ties in derogation of ties created voluntarily by loving effort." He explained what he feels is at stake:

> . . . Analogizing race to family is a potent rhetorical move used to challenge those, like me, who are animated by a liberal, individualistic, and universal ethos which is skeptical of, if not hostile to, the particularisms—national, ethnic, religious, and racial—which seem to have grown so strong recently, even in those arenas, such as major cosmopolitan universities, where one might have expected their demise.

So uncompromising was Kennedy's opposition to expressions of racial affinity that he even criticized Yale Law School professor Stephen L. Carter, a thoughtful and persuasive critic of affirmative action and other racial policies, for writing about the pleasure he and his wife take in inviting black students to their home at Christmas, feeling "a deep emotional connection to them, through our blackness . . . a reminder of the bright and supportive side of solidarity." Kennedy's response was that

> . . . in the mind, heart, and soul of a teacher there should be no stratification of students such that, on grounds of racial kinship, a teacher feels closer to certain pupils than others. No teacher should view certain students as his racial "brothers and sisters" while viewing the others as, well, mere students. Every student should be free of the worry that, because of his or her race, he or she will have less of an opportunity to benefit from what a teacher has to offer.

Kennedy is rigorously rational in his public speaking and writing; he eschews colorful or emotive language. So, coming from him, the phrase "mind, heart, and soul of a teacher" signaled his deep conviction that being a good teacher means more than performing "official duties" such as answering students' queries and keeping regular office hours. In his lecture, he lauded some of his own white teachers—John McCune, Eric Foner, Sanford Levinson, Owen Fiss—whose keen interest in teaching and in him had changed his life and nourished friendships that continue. In effect, he paid tribute to a dimension of civil society that can't be regulated but makes all the difference to individual growth and social health.

Kennedy anticipated two likely objections to his argument: As long as a teacher performs his or her "official duties" equally well for all students, none are deprived. And since racism is a fact of life, black students need and deserve whatever knowledge, guidance, and assistance a black professor can provide—not in "kinship" but to meet race-neutral, universal moral standards. Kennedy warned that when a teacher affirms racial kinship, "I find it inconceivable that there will be no seepage from the sphere of the personal into the sphere of the professional." Students invited to a professor's home are enjoying an opportunity that may well "be reflected, for instance, in letters of recommendation to Judge So-and-So and Law Firm Partner Such-and-Such" and in the students' own perceptions and feelings of the pedagogical relationship. Only a clear moral duty, not color-coded "kinship," should animate a teacher, he argued, explaining the difference:

Am I demanding that teachers be blind to race? No, I am not. . . . They should be keenly aware, for instance, that . . . the dominant form of racial kinship in American life . . . [is] mobilized on behalf of whites. . . . Consider the case . . . in which white students are receiving considerable attention from teachers, while black students are being widely and wrongly ignored. In this case, it would be morally correct for a professor . . . to reach out with special vigor to black students. . . . Note, though, that the basis for this outreach is not racial kinship. Rather, the outreach is justified on grounds of distributive justice. . . . Under this rationale, white teachers are at least as morally obligated to address the problem as are black or other professors.

Broadening his argument from the nature of teachers' obligations to that of social obligations more generally, Kennedy argued that "difficulties that disproportionately afflict black Americans are not 'black problems' whose solution are the special responsibilities of black people. [These problems'] solution or amelioration are the responsibility of us all, irrespective of race." He celebrated whites, from Elijah Lovejoy, who was murdered in 1837 for opposing slavery, to 1960s civil rights activists Andrew Goodman, Michael Schwerner, and others who lost their lives struggling to secure blacks' civil rights out of a sense of moral obligation, not racial kinship. "Against this history," he concluded, "I see no reason why paying homage to the struggle for racial justice must entail any sort of racially-stratified loyalty. Indeed, this history suggests the opposite." The way to oppose racism is to renounce racial loyalty—which is chimerical and only compounds racism itself—and to honor and reward "loving effort" guided by a universal morality that can animate everyone from foster parents to civil rights activists.

At Columbia, many of Kennedy's listeners thought him hopelessly if not willfully naive about the bitter experiences of blacks, who had long heard whites mouthing such pieties. New York University law professor Derrick Bell had already charged portentously in the *New York Times* that Kennedy "is willing to speak for whites"—which meant that, by Bell's lights, he was a race traitor. Responding to Kennedy at Columbia, Manning Marable, a professor of history and African-American studies there, acknowledged that blackness in America is not a primordial or mystical bond but a "social construct," a product of racism. Still, he asked, given the depth and prevalence of white racism, was there not—and shouldn't there continue to be—a black community born of shared endurance, resistance, and memory? Another listener, a black man with an activist's mien and an Caribbean accent, made the same argument, but in language more damning of Kennedy. In Sandel's class at

Harvard, a black student responded much as Marable had, asking Kennedy to agree that the shared ordeal of being black in America bonds and obligates blacks to one another.

Kennedy's responses recapitulated what he had said in his lecture:

> A brute fact [of racism] does not dictate the proper human response to it. . . . Blacks should insist, as did Martin Luther King, Jr., that acting with moral propriety is itself a glorious goal. In seeking to attain that goal, blacks should be attuned not only to the all-too-human cruelties and weaknesses of others, but . . . as well . . . of themselves. . . . Unless inhibited, every person and group will tend to gravitate toward beliefs and practices that are self-aggrandizing.

Kennedy was warning, in effect, that his critics' invocations of black solidarity are only half-answers to racist oppression. They leave unanswered the question of whether *any* group or society can sustain its members' dignity, much less respect it in others, if it stops taking universal principles seriously. Ultimately, Kennedy said, there really is no substitute for a classical, universal liberal morality. He warned that "national" solidarities are as suspect as explicitly racial ones but acknowledged, in response to a question from me, that loyalty to the American republic is justifiable to the extent that citizenship here is based not on mystical ties in "blood and soil" but in the republic's commitments to implement race-transcendent ideals. That is precisely why "millions of people come here from all over the world," he said.

Yet Kennedy wanted to preserve a tension between even the most benign loyalty to America and higher obligations to human rights around the world. Sometimes, as in the Vietnam War, patriotism cannot be reconciled with higher obligations—and never mind that Lyndon Johnson presented the war as a moral crusade against an immoral ideology. While communism was a perversion of universal morality, Johnson was wrong because America's "crusade" was inseparable from militarism and capitalist greed, which coexist uneasily with higher liberal aspirations. At Columbia, some of Kennedy's nonwhite listeners asserted that militarism and greed are indeed inextricable from liberalism itself, and, moreover, that there is something quintessentially "white" about that corruption of universal standards. Kennedy denied that the connection was inevitable, even though he had protested the war.

A stronger case for maintaining nonwhite subcultures in a classical liberal society came, ironically, from Kennedy's white interlocutor at Harvard, Michael Sandel. He asked whether Jackie Robinson had been wrong to say, while recounting his experience of breaking baseball's color bar, that he had taken "pride in the pride which my people took in me." Isn't there an important value, asked Sandel, as had Marable at Columbia, in honoring one's membership in a group that has been shaped by and forged in oppression? Going even further, Sandel asked whether people may not have enduring obligations to ancient subcultures which, while not avowedly liberal and universal, nurture individual dignity and moral obligation in their members. Where else did Kennedy think young people would acquire and affirm dignity? Certainly not only in a liberal marketplace of goods and ideas.

If Kennedy was taking liberal humanism to extremes of abstraction in his battle against liberal racism, Sandel was pushing a little the other way. He suggested that there really is no such thing as a morally "unencumbered self," dear though that notion might be to some liberal Constitutional scholars and free-market economists. But Kennedy resisted even Jackie Robinson's seemingly harmless notion of racial kinship. He recalled how members of an NAACP audience had objected when presidential candidate Ross Perot addressed them as "you people"; yet, the next day, the same listeners referred to themselves as "our people," showing, in Kennedy's view, how provisional—indeed, shallow—racial or ethnic "peoplehood" in America can be.

But just how provisional is the experience of racial kinship for Kennedy himself? Thereby hangs a tale of the creative tension between parochial nurture and liberal aspiration in America, a tension which Kennedy and many others have known. To learn how difficult and important the right balance can be, Kennedy's own story is a good place to start.

◆ An American Universalist

In his professional and public life, Kennedy lives uncompromisingly by the principles he enunciated in the lectures. When some Harvard Law School students invited a little-known member of the Nation of Islam to speak at the school in 1993—a year after Farrakhan lieutenant Khalid Muhammad's infamous anti-Semitic rant at Kean College in New Jersey—Kennedy attended the speech at some of his own students' request. "For a while," he recalled later,

> the guy didn't say anything blatant; it was all innuendo, insinuation. But there came a point, after about thirty minutes, when he said something—I've forgotten it, frankly—in which the implication was sufficiently clear so that I felt like I had to do something. There was a group of mainly Jewish students in the back holding up these placards, with messages like "Hate is not welcome here at Harvard," and I went up to one—I think at first the guy thought I was trying to take his placard away from him, and then he understood that I just wanted to hold it—and I just walked down the aisle to the front and held it up. Muhammad was still speaking, and I didn't stop the show, but I felt that it was important to show that it wasn't just the group of students in the back who felt this way. I don't think it was that big a deal.
>
> Some students came up to me afterward and said, "Thanks." Others thought I had acted wrongly, and one said, "This guy didn't really say anything anti-Semitic." I said, "Frankly, my response to you is just what it would be when David Duke's people claim that he doesn't say anything antiblack nowadays." (Conversation with author, June, 1996)

At around that time, Kennedy "went public" in defense of interracial adoptions, which the National Association of Black Social Workers was equating with "genocide" on the grounds that such adoptions deprived black infants of "culturally consistent" environments. The NABSW supported regulations that would leave black infants who'd been abandoned by their parents languishing in hospitals until other black families could be found to adopt them. But—contrary to what a liberal racist might presume—more white families than black stand ready to adopt black children. Apparently, white love is as threatening as white hate to those who would rather treat a race as a "family" than respect individuals' cross-racial moral choices.

The NABSW induced New York State to adopt "cultural consistency" regulations and got Ohio senator Howard Metzenbaum to propose a "Multiethnic Placement Act" that would keep black "boarder babies" in hospitals at least until concerted efforts had been made to find them black homes. Kennedy endorsed efforts to recruit more black families, as a group called Miracle Workers does in New York. But he knew that any delay in placing abandoned infants with loving families retards their development. What especially galled him into opposing the Metzenbaum bill was its incorporation of a principle of racial matching driven by what he called "ugly and destructive" sentiments such as "antiwhite racism, a rigid determinism according to which people of one race are simply incapable of fully loving and empathizing with people of another race, . . . and a tendency to view black children as hostages that can justifiably be used to advance the ideology and bureaucratic power of the NABSW."

When Kennedy made this case to one of his classes during a wrenching discussion of the problem, a black student responded, "The reason you take that position is that you don't believe in diversity." Thirty years ago, an equally provocative charge might have been, "You don't believe in racial integration"—the very thing Kennedy was now affirming, as he had in his Trilling lecture by endorsing "interracial intimacy of the most profound sort." So he turned the tables on his student:

> Let me stop you right there. I think that's an interesting point you just made. Couldn't it be that *you're* a conservative, and that *I'm* saying, "Let a hundred flowers bloom"? I think it can be great to

have a family of many colors. I'm for new ways of thinking, new formations, nontraditional family models. Isn't *that* "diversity"? Suppose that, in a supermarket, we see a family with differently colored parents and kids go through the line. You're going to be upset by that, and I'm not.

The student was already upset, and the rest of the class's response was mixed, if muted. "I think the majority sentiment was with me, but people who felt that way were very quiet," Kennedy reflected later. "Clearly the people who feel most confident these days are the race-matching people. I don't care. When Clint Bollick of the [conservative] Institute for Justice contacted me about signing on to a Texas case involving white foster parents who were defending their custody of a black child from a challenge by the birth mother who had abandoned the infant, I said, 'Yes.' "

Teaching a special summer course for legal practitioners, Kennedy asked the class, as he does in his book *Race, Crime, and the Law,* whether it was racist of Congress to mandate Draconian sentences for the possession of crack-cocaine, which blacks disproportionately use, but not for the less dangerous powder cocaine, which is used more by whites. The legislation didn't mention race, Kennedy noted; Congress's "rush to judgment" might be "hysterical, it might be unwise, it might be counterproductive," he said, but mightn't its harsh crack penalties reflect a sincere belief that crack is more lethal and socially disruptive than powder? Didn't it matter that that belief and harsher sentences were endorsed by Harlem congressman Charles Rangel, who sponsored the legislation, and by many others in the Congressional Black Caucus who voted for it?

Kennedy kept on pitting humanism against racialism. "People say there's no reason for Alan Bakke [the white medical-school applicant who sued successfully against an affirmative-action policy which he believed had denied him admission] to feel discriminated against because he's being disadvantaged for a larger common good," he told me. "I say, let's talk that way, then, about a black [motorist] being stopped by a cop. Your skin color is simply incidental to a larger problem [of black crime, which harms blacks more than whites]; you shouldn't feel discriminated against, either. [But] if that doesn't satisfy me as a driver—assuming, of course, that the officer is polite and just checking records—why should it satisfy Bakke?"

Kennedy almost always poses such questions as rigorously as he did in the Trilling lecture. But late in 1996, in a review for the *Los Angeles Times,* he characterized Johnnie Cochran's *Journey for Justice* as a manipulative, preening account of his life and work that reeked of emotional and intellectual dishonesty. That prompted Kennedy's Harvard colleagues Leon Higginbotham, Charles Ogletree, Jr., and David Wilkins to charge in the same newspaper that he had "unfairly maligned Cochran's honesty and integrity." Does Kennedy just play devil's advocate when he challenges the conventional racial wisdom? Or is Randall Kennedy deracinated, or, worse, a race traitor—supporting "white power" against blacks and other "people of color"?

The last question was posed pointedly—indeed, furiously—for the first time in 1989, when he published, in the *Harvard Law Review* a magisterial assessment of the work of "critical race theorists" such as Derrick Bell, Richard Delgado, and Mari Matsuda. The controversy it sparked illuminated the cultural and philosophical gap between liberal racists and those whom Kennedy considers true liberals.

In the essay "Racial Critiques of Legal Academia," Kennedy summarized critical race theorists' contention that nonwhites' historic and continuing subordination gives them special insights and wisdom, leaving whites "entitled to less 'standing' in race-relations law discourse than academics of color." He noted that these theorists also believe that simply being nonwhite "should serve [applicants for student admissions and faculty positions] as a positive credential for purposes of evaluating their work" and that if nonwhites are underrepresented or ranked poorly in academies, that is due largely to "prejudiced decisions by white academics," not to a dearth of fully qualified nonwhites, which would reflect a confluence of other factors. More fatefully, he noted, critical race theorists insist that rigorous rational analysis, rooted in classical liberal conceptions of empirical proof and of individual rights and responsibilities, is "white" thinking, and that legal scholarship and processes must be changed to accommodate the collective consciousness of nonwhites, using literary fables whose truths are deemed vital, even when they can't be established by traditional scholarship.

In his essay, Kennedy disagreed, of course. He believes in "a liberal, individualistic, and universal ethos that is skeptical of, if not hostile to, the particularisms—national, ethnic, religious, and racial—which seem to have grown so strong recently. . . ." He fully acknowledged the persistence of white disdain for nonwhites' intellectual efforts. But he also exposed the intellectual failings in "critical race" narratives, which tend, he wrote, "to evade or suppress complications that render their conclusions problematic. Stated bluntly, they fail to support persuasively their claims of racial exclusion or their claims that nonwhite legal academic scholars produce a racially distinctive brand of valuable scholarship" that is beyond comprehension by whites.

Far from being a problem just for legal scholars, Kennedy warned, critical race theory lends support to "certain educators who conclude, on the basis of flimsy evidence, that there exists a 'black learning style' that distinguishes black children from the children of other racial groups. Left unchallenged, this tendency will seep into the culture at large and reinforce beliefs about 'natural' divisions that have, for too long, constricted our imaginations." The seepage is already evident in many public-school curricula. Moreover, as Daniel Aaron has observed, the most effective and enduring black writers, from Richard Wright to Albert Murray, have wrestled with the lure of black racialism and the challenge of universalism, finding their own moral centers, as Aaron noted, by identifying their predicament as blacks with the American predicament. Are they their race's traitors, or redeemers?

Kennedy's article provoked bitter, highly personal responses. At a panel sponsored by the Association of American

Law Schools, a critical race theorist likened Kennedy to a Tonto figure, the fictional Indian whose loyalty to the Lone Ranger set him apart from, if not against, his tribe. Derrick Bell told Kennedy that he shouldn't have published his article because "we need you on our side, not in our way." The writer Jonathan Wiener characterized him in *The Nation* as the voice of a white-bread legal establishment—no small irony, since Kennedy himself is a member of the magazine's editorial board. Kennedy told me he found the irony somewhat amusing—and instructive:

> I thought, "How stupid." Here I am, a social democrat who would redistribute wealth in ways that would put me on the left of the Democratic Party, yet, simply because of this, I'm called a conservative. My younger sister was at Howard Law School at the time, and some of her fellow students told her, "Your brother's so conservative," all because of reaction to this piece. My fate isn't so different from that of [the black sociologist] William Julius Wilson, who was called a conservative just because he said that race was declining in significance as a cause of black poverty. Ironically, the self-styled "radicals" who attack me are the real conservatives. What about experimentation? What about open-mindedness?

The attacks in *The Nation* and some other left-wing periodicals showed how thoroughly the once-universalist left had succumbed to its racism, leaving people like Kennedy as holdouts for humanism, at least on that end of the political spectrum. But that did not turn holdouts like Kennedy into conservatives. "When some on the right viewed the attacks as a signal that I was a possible recruit, I thought, 'This is an interesting kind of dynamic that creates a Thomas Sowell [the sociologist and partisan conservative columnist],' " Kennedy told me. "I've never responded to either side. I'm somewhat at fault for that; it's an intellectual's responsibility to respond, unless an attack is in bad faith or the critic is a crank. But I didn't like the feeling of having to choose between 'right' and 'left,' with one side viewing me as a renegade, the other as a convert."

◆ A Child of Black Struggle

As it happens, Kennedy knows what it's like to be stopped unjustly by cops and what it's like to be black in America. Born in Columbia, South Carolina, in 1956, he moved to Washington, D.C. in infancy with his parents, who, he recalls, considered themselves refugees from "a white-supremacist South that they thought would strangle them and their kids. My father thought he would get into trouble there," owing to a couple of scrapes with abusive policemen and shopkeepers. One of Kennedy's indelible memories is of watching his proud father accommodate Jim Crow etiquette to protect his family when police pulled him over during a drive back to South Carolina in 1965:

> The cop said, "Boy, where ya comin' from? Where ya goin?" My father said, "Sir, I'm coming from Washington, D.C. I'm going to South Carolina." He was not foolhardy; he knew what could happen if he answered as he felt like answering, and he had my mother and us kids in the car. I remember spending the summer of 1964 with my Aunt Lillian in Columbia, when the state closed its parks rather than desegregate them; I clearly remember climbing the stairs to the black section of the movie theater. I remember being called "nigger."
>
> I know black history inside and out; I am thoroughly familiar with the various sectors of the black population, and I don't have any problem with my blackness whatsoever. I know and love Gospel music; I've been in more than a few Baptist churches where people ran down aisles and shouted. Some people are taken aback when I say that I am in favor of transracial adoption and try to hit me with, "You're naive; you don't know about white racism." But I know.

How, then, can Kennedy remain a staunch universalist when many blacks are deciding that integration has failed and are withdrawing into racial particularism and proportionalism? He insists that liberal racialism is nothing but a moral and spiritual dead end and that it cannot be reconciled with moral or intellectual integrity. But how did he come by that insight and his passion for defending it?

The answer has something to do with disciplined aspiration at the core of the black culture he knew, which placed an almost religious emphasis on balancing personal moral responsibility with universalism. It also has something to do with an experience of racial integration where white friendships were natural and deeply rewarding.

Kennedy's father, a postal worker, and his mother, a public school teacher, scrimped and saved until they could move from an apartment in southeast Washington, D.C. to a row house and, as he entered adolescence, to a freestanding house in the northwest neighborhood of Takoma Park, which at the time was half white.

Education was the end-all and be-all. Respectability was ultra-important. My parents were not interested in "success" but in doing your best. They weren't overawed by wealth or even achievement. A person who takes care of their family, stays out of trouble, and can be counted on—those are the things that matter. Some of our neighbors were garbagemen. Fine! Wonderful neighbors! In my parents' eyes, the man who goes to work every day and takes care of his property doesn't have to take a back step to anyone in the world.

We attended Asbury United Methodist Church, an old, solidly working-class congregation. The ministers were my heroes. I was very active; I read the liturgy and went to Camp Atwater in Worcester, Massachusetts, a black summer camp. My house was religious, culturally conservative—no cursing, smoking, or drinking.

I became a father relatively late partly because I was daunted by what I had seen in my parents' incredible generosity and single-mindedness. We kids came first; it was as simple as that. There was this total investment. In that way, we grew up "above our station," even though they were not wealthy at all. It's why my brother's a judge [in District of Columbia Superior Court], I'm a law professor, and my sister's a lawyer.

Something else accounts for the Kennedy children's remarkable ascent: the fullness of the integration they experienced, both through their parents' example and in the neighborhood of Kennedy's youth. In 1960, Kennedy's mother became the first—and for many years was the only—black teacher in a Chevy Chase (Maryland) elementary school, all of whose students were white. But even more important than her experience was his own among playmates of all colors, in Takoma Park.

It was a *wonderful* place to grow up! I learned to play tennis in the park. I played in the National Junior Tennis Tournament. My sister played the violin. My elementary and junior high schools were integrated. I've always gone to school with a good number of white kids and had a lot of white friends.

My brother [who is five years older] went to Princeton because of a white guy who went to Coolidge High School with him, a guy named Harvey. When Harvey told him he was applying to Princeton, my brother said, "Princeton doesn't want people like me"—this was in 1966—and Harvey said, "Nah, nah, things are changing; Princeton is *looking* for people like you." Harvey's encouragement made the difference. My brother got in on a big scholarship. And because he went to Princeton and did well, I and my sister went, too. The idea of having white friends through all this was not a big deal, but, in some ways I never thought about self-consciously, it played a role in my thinking.

Kennedy didn't follow his brother to Coolidge High School, which was going downhill quickly in all the predictable urban ways. He got into Washington's exclusive, private St. Albans School, where he had fine teachers and made close white friends. Still, he felt a stab of recognition one night in 1995 when he turned on C-Span and saw that the Coolidge High auditorium was the site of a lurid antiwhite hate-fest on the eve of the Million Man March. At Coolidge, diatribes against whites were delivered by people who wouldn't be on the podium at the Mall the next day. "I saw that," Kennedy moans. "I watched it. Malik Abdul Shabbazz [one of the event's ring-leaders] was in my sister's class at Howard Law School. Oh, was that *horrible*!"

It was also symptomatic of what had become of the kind of integration Kennedy had known. He sighed when I mentioned that David Dinkins, the former mayor of New York, had once gotten teary while describing his friendship with a now-deceased Jewish man, saying, "We were so close that one didn't know what the other was":

If David Dinkins made that comment in one of my classes now, people would roll their eyes and think it's ridiculous. In an article on "unconscious racism," Chuck Lawrence [a critical race theorist] quotes a white person saying, "I never notice the difference between my friends," and he writes that that person is deluded. But I can imagine a person saying that and it being a quite decent, thoroughgoing thing. What he's saying is, "Of course I know that you're a different color and that things may be different for you, but there's a deeper thing going on here; you're a child of God, I'm a child of God." And of course I believe that and embrace that.

Are such friendships indispensable to learning that racialist thinking is wrong? "No, I don't think so, really," Kennedy answered. "Some of the kids who are the most 'group-istic' grew up in integrated environments and are rebelling against that." Were their encounters with integration mandated and force-fed, not embraced naturally, as Dinkins's and Kennedy's had been? "Maybe, but part of what you end up believing [depends on] what ideas grabbed you. I think that, early on, integrationist notions grabbed me. I was only eight years old when Martin Luther King gave his 'I have a dream' speech, but it's the ideology that I grew up with."

Kennedy's mother kept that faith not just by reporting to her school every day and taking home a paycheck; she embodied and implemented it. Today's legal and pedagogical racism, so sweeping in asserting the immutability of black/white differences, derides her faith nearly as much as did the old, white opposition to integration itself. "That's my problem with some people's romantic notion of speaking for all people of color," Kennedy says.

They write as if it's really not a dilemma you have to think hard about. I'm saying there are actually dilemmas out here, real choices facing people of goodwill. What is the best way to allocate voting power? What is the best way to organize public education? What kind of social order do we want? What *is* racial equality? Solving these demands knowledge, a command of facts and figures. Instead, people like Bell are saying, "Jeez, Dred Scott was really wrong, racism is really bad." I say, "Have we finished with that?" They do not want to finish that conversation.

Liberal racists will take this last complaint as an affront and as proof that Kennedy is discounting the strong racial kinship that made the Asbury United Methodist Church and his summer camp such wonderful places to grow up. But he is posing a far different challenge: In his view, growing up means outgrowing temptations to resort to racial kinship as the central preoccupation and organizing principle of one's life. It means broadening the range of one's friendships and commitments, even as one sustains and enriches communal institutions that are rooted deeply but aspiring broadly. Kennedy thinks that blacks need to emphasize the latter in their public life right now and to resist more than ever before the temptation to withdraw into the fantasy of a separate racial destiny. Truly to grow up is to discover that it *is* a fantasy.

◆ A Sojourn on the Right

No one would ever mistake the economist and social critic Glenn Loury for a deracinated black man. A native of Chicago's South Side whose father worked in the stockyards, Loury looks physically as many would expect a son of the solid, stolid black working class to look: Where Kennedy is trim, athletic, well-tailored, and horn-rimmed, Loury, a professor of economics at Boston University and the holder of a prestigious fellowship at the international Econometric Society, is heavyset and properly yet indifferently attired. A rigorous, lucid public speaker, he nevertheless conveys a grounded black urban sensibility, by turns preacherly and colloquial.

More important than the two men's appearance and

manner of address, of course, is their intellectual provenance. While Kennedy has rejected black race loyalty and the leftist "identity politics" of *The Nation* for a more vital liberal center, Loury has left behind conservative hypocrisy about "color blindness" and the preoccupation with black pathology at the neoconservative *Commentary* magazine, for which he wrote frequently until breaking with it over its support for *Bell Curve* author Charles Murray. He also resigned from a fellowship at the conservative American Enterprise Institute to protest its sponsorship of Dinesh D'Souza's *The End of Racism,* which was widely condemned for emphasizing the role of black cultural "pathologies" in black alienation from the larger society. But, like Kennedy, Loury doesn't find liberal racism attractive:

> I came to conservatism in the first place because I was really angry with liberals—disgusted, disappointed, tired with their keeping their heads in the sand, unable or unwilling to look at how their best intentions had gone awry, particularly as it had to do with black folk. I'd point at that, and a ton of bricks would fall on my head; it all went back to the Moynihan Report and people's accusations that if you endorsed it you were giving aid and comfort to the enemy.
>
> When I came to Harvard in 1982, I tried to become editor of the *Review of Black Political Economy.* I was the most qualified for that job. Those people did not come close to letting me edit it, because I had discredited myself as a loyal black person. I was still the same person, except I had written some articles saying that everything is not right with the civil rights movement. (Conversation with author, June, 1996)

What Loury admired in neoconservatives, he wrote recently, was "their willingness to confront the patronizing relativism which white liberals seemed inevitably to bring to questions of race. [Liberals were] blind to the desperate need of the 'victims' to take responsibility for their own lives." Neoconservatives seemed to take blacks seriously enough to criticize them; when Loury began writing for Irving Kristol's journal, *The Public Interest,* he thought he was joining a community based in the concern for poor blacks which the sociologist Nathan Glazer and U.S. Senator Daniel Patrick Moynihan had demonstrated, albeit in ways that had angered liberals and leftists.

But eventually Loury concluded that neoconservatives and conservatives are more interested in showing where liberals went wrong than they are in treating the urban poor as fellow Americans—an approach that, in his view, would require a national mobilization driven by transracial, humanist principles such as those Kennedy defends. Conservatives' sponsorship of *The Bell Curve* and *The End of Racism,* which both went in the opposite direction and beyond, were wake-up calls for Loury, and he was instrumental in discrediting them. But he had been made to feel uncomfortable in conservative circles:

> At one meeting, I said, is it really the case that every possible acknowledgment of the reality of race is a totally corrupting thing? About those who say yes, the kindest thing I can say is, they're confused. Sometimes they just have a *schtick* about color-coding, and they're milking the opposition to it for all it's worth. When I would dissent, people would say, "I thought you were on our side, Glenn." It was like, "He's deviating a little bit."

At a meeting convened by William Bennett in 1995 to discuss the "culture wars" conservatives were waging against liberals on several fronts, Loury brought up the problem of conservative finger-pointing at blacks.

> I mentioned the antiblack campaign rhetoric of some Republicans running in state races, against, for example, "the sewer of New Orleans." I said, Look, if you will stand up and do the right thing on this and the *Bell Curve,* I'll keep denouncing liberal abuses, correcting, instructing, hectoring. I want to know how much black pathology language do we really need to get our work done here? How much demonization of these people? We want to try juveniles as adults. What's next, twelve-year-olds? You don't have to be a "society-is-to-blame" liberal to recognize that there's stuff going on in inner cities that doesn't give people

choices. You don't have to like liberal solutions. I don't either. What's not acceptable is writing these people off and making them into objects you run against.

Well, they were bored. Bill Bennett was *bored*. They didn't want to talk about this. They were talking about campaigns against movie producers, record stuff, which is fine with me, you know, but there was no item on the agenda about what I was trying to raise.

Late in 1996, after *Commentary* editor Norman Podhoretz announced that neoconservatism was no longer distinguishable from conservatism, Loury announced his break with both in *Commonquest,* a black-Jewish journal, in the Fall 1996 issue:

Many neoconservatives marched for racial justice thirty years ago. Then, the demons were clear; they are less so now. But you cannot tell me that what now transpires in ghetto America does not constitute a great injustice to those hundreds of thousands of youngsters who never got a chance. Conservative ideologues may rest content with being right about liberals having been wrong. But, if they are to remain true to their own roots, these intellectuals who grew up in Brooklyn or on the Lower East Side . . . should want more. If neoconservatism has ceased to exist, then its cause of death is a failure of moral imagination.

I asked Loury whether there aren't some conservatives who agree with him about the importance of reaching for poor urban blacks as fellow Americans, even if that means mobilizing resources. He cited several who share his concern, but added:

There's no school of thought within conservatism saying this, no reckoning with the problem. [Republican former congressman and vice-presidential candidate] Jack Kemp believes in dynamic capitalism, and that's great, but, to me, that's a question about method, not values. A person has to be willing to adjust their method and be driven by their values. . . . I am the first to say the old liberal way has not worked. But there's no way around the fact that the first few years of these [poor, inner-city] kids' lives

are critical; we are either gonna take them away from incompetent parents, or we're gonna enrich the environments they're in
so they have a possibility of getting on the track of opportunity.
Now, that's gonna cost money or something. It's gonna cost
freedom; if we take 'em away from parents, it's gonna be intru-
sive, and we're gonna have to substitute something for that. Or
it's gonna require a tremendous upswelling of voluntarism and
engagement across the board.

The conservative problem with race is as obvious as its solution. The problem is that a significant minority of the movement's members and leaders regard poor inner-city blacks
less as fellow Americans than as aliens—so much so, in fact,
that they can't seem to stop generating (and subsidizing)
genetic theories that reinforce their misguided contempt. The
solution, which honorable conservatives must help find, involves doing much more to combat discrimination and to
help struggling, inner-city blacks enrich the first critical years
of children's lives. But Loury knows that few conservatives are
likely to do anything serious along those lines.

If some conservatives treated Randall Kennedy as a potential recruit, however wrongly, mightn't liberals try to welcome
Loury as one of them? Some have reached out, but it is hard
to count on liberals' enduring commitment to a passionate,
visibly "authentic" black man who refuses to abandon the classical liberal principles which liberal racism has betrayed. Loury
recalls the discomfort he caused when he told a group of liberals that they ignore or misconstrue inner-city dilemmas as
much as conservatives do. At a friend's behest, he spoke at a
conference on racism in 1995 at the liberal Hubert Humphrey
Institute in Minneapolis:

It was exactly what I had feared—a "world conference" on racial
and ethnic inequality that was politically correct. On a panel with
[defenders of liberal orthodoxy such as] Barbara Bergmann and
Manning Marable, I said any national effort to deal with the
underclass simply has to be built on transracial, humanistic principles. It can't be about reparations, or log-rolling in the Democratic Party, where you get your special [racial] thing by giving

them your votes. It's about what kind of people are we as Americans, about what kind of commonality we can build upon.

Many liberals and leftists in the audience, preferring, as always, imaginary purity to actual progress, were uneasy with Loury's insistence on "commonality." Some became even more uncomfortable when he noted that applying humanist principles means making hard judgments about the damage done not just by racism and the economy but by failures of individual responsibility:

> I said, "What are you going to do about welfare mothers who don't take responsibility for their children, and about criminal felons? You have to be prepared to make judgments." And we got into the testing thing, and I said, "Look, don't be in denial; there are real differences in the cognitive abilities as they are expressed between blacks and whites in this country. Those test scores are not a figment of anybody's imagination. They're not about bias— I'm not saying bias doesn't exist—and not about mean-spirited scientists trying to malign people—even though there's that, too. The story is that the developed capacities of human beings differ by race. I don't believe it's genetic; I think you can easily give plausible accounts of how this could happen. But it's a fact. Okay?
> *"So let's talk about who's going to read to these kids; let's talk about the verbal stimulation of kids as they develop their linguistic abilities.* How come these public libraries at the corners of housing projects aren't overflowing? I mean, people have different styles, and I don't care if it's Barney or computer games; but let's talk about the development of the abilities of these children."

Loury was raising the "culture of poverty" problem which liberals such as Andrew Hacker and Benjamin DeMott deride or duck. In 1990, the *New York Times* ran a fifty-year-old photograph of the Stone Avenue branch of the Brooklyn Public Library, now surrounded by public housing projects in the borough's poor, black Brownsville section. Fifty years earlier, the story noted, poor kids such as the literary critic Alfred Kazin and *Commentary* editor Norman Podhoretz had spent hours there, reading books they could never otherwise have obtained; an old photograph showed scores of children lined up outside because the building was already crowded with children reading. (Liberal government hasn't abandoned the Stone Avenue branch since then; thanks to Mayor Dinkins's visionary operations director Harvey Robins, all local library branches, whose schedules had been constricted since the fiscal crisis of the mid-1970s, are open six days a week. Yet even when the Stone Avenue branch is open and ready to serve, its children's section is almost deserted.) Shown the old photograph, branch librarian Robert Visceglia said, "We don't get lines like that anymore. It looks like they were giving something away for free." Well, they were—and are still. The question is why there are so few takers. The problem isn't racism or capitalism—at least no more so than in the 1930s, when the parents of many of the children in the old photograph were poor and illiterate. If anything, Brownsville's politics then was anticapitalist and antiracist enough to demand the construction and racial integration of new public housing. That won't solve the new problem.

Loury's listeners couldn't acknowledge the importance of moral responsibility in his discussion of test results. When he noted that standardized tests recorded kids' deficiencies in reading, "People said, 'Oh, the SAT doesn't measure these abilities well,' or 'The counselors channel the kids into the wrong thing.' I didn't want to argue with them about that. I simply said, 'Okay, let me concede that to you. There's that. But then there's also this problem of culture, of reading to kids. Can we talk about *this* now?' "

Some couldn't. They complained that such talk plays into the hands of conservatives who want to exclude blacks, not uplift them. Yet Loury had struck a nerve.

Afterwards, people came up to me. . . . There was one woman who said, "I've heard you speak, I've always had a problem with you, but I realize tonight that I had never really listened to you before."

I think I am saying it differently now than I used to. I used to say, "Here's what's wrong with the traditional black leadership."

Now I say, "Do you know what these conservatives are up to?" I use a line about black ju-jitsu politics, the strategy of saying, "I'm weak, therefore I'm strong. I use your strength against you by saying that we blacks haven't accomplished anything; we're weak, therefore, you owe us, because you treated us badly." Well, the jig is up on that, I say, because conservatives answer, "You people don't have the equipment to function in modern society. You're barbaric, you're incompetent, you're dumb." And it's not just whispered; it's trotted out with great detail and sophistication. And people are listening.

It just won't work for liberals to point to prisons overflowing with young black men and then accuse the system of injustice. People will say, "What about the individuals who were raped, bludgeoned, robbed?" We have to persuade a majority of our fellow citizens to get with us in a program that they can see is consistent with their values and their interests. That is not a racial undertaking. That is a civic undertaking. It's about what kind of country is the United States of America.

What kind of country *is* the United States of America, if conservatives succeed by playing the divisive politics Loury describes? How enduringly, abidingly racist is it? "Well, I look at NBA playoffs, and I see Michael Jordan," he told me. "I look at the statistics on interracial marriage and there is no doubt that there has been deep, deep change. [An important study by Douglas Besharov of the American Enterprise Institute shows that, of all marriages in 1990 in which one or both persons were black, about 6 percent are black-white marriages— a fivefold increase since 1960. And, Besharov finds, the rate of black-white marriages is now increasing even more rapidly.] White kids listen to rap music, and there's a lot that's wrong with rap music, but it shows the energy, centrality, the dynamism that comes out of black America."

Such observations have prompted Loury to consider something that liberals accuse Randall Kennedy of neglecting: the communal—and, therefore, racial—dimensions of moral responsibility. "Obsession about racial difference is a threat to American democracy, and yet assimilation is a threat to identity," Loury says. "People do need a protected cultural envi-

ronment within which to create individualism itself." Loury
felt a deep sense of belonging as he walked across the Washington Mall during the Million Man March, confirming Michael
Sandel's assertion that there's no such thing as an "unencumbered" individual—that people need to be raised in some subculture. Yet in choosing the national Mall, not Harlem, for the
march Farrakhan was affirming, if only unwittingly, that
American civic culture operates on two tiers: People are nurtured in varied subcultures, but they transcend them at times
to participate in a shared civic life in which all agree to curb
racial and ethnic affinities in order to treat people as individuals, not group delegates.

I proposed to Loury that blacks, always the most excluded
from the upper tier, had nevertheless kept the two-tiered balance best of all. When Rosa Parks quietly refused to give up
her seat on that segregated public bus in Montgomery in
1955, she expressed a desire to embrace and redeem society,
not to rebuff it as inherently, eternally racist. The solid black
working class from which Loury came had kept that faith, too,
often with greater fortitude and idealism than do whites who
tout civil society now. Such blacks, I said, *are* the most
American of us all, because of what they go through to sustain
the balance of parochialism and universalism.

"I agree with you totally," Loury replied, "but the bottom
tier was gritty, intimate, personal, and immediate, while, for
most people, the larger thing involved abstraction, belief,
faith.

Blacks had to believe we would overcome even when there was
scant reason to believe we would: People had to go to court to
fight for antilynching laws and debate the meaning of the Constitution just to sit in integrated trains and buses. People who
thought that progressive politics would be transformative had to
deal with the fact that it was incomplete. And faith in the larger
society is waning now under the pressures of postmodern, multicultural critiques of liberalism. The upper tier of the model is
something people have lost confidence in. Say that this is a
melting pot, and people laugh. They say it's a salad bowl. What

are we all supposed to believe in? There's no clear message anymore, from liberals or conservatives.

For blacks, faith in the larger American society arose because
the alternative was despair. I was at a conference with Charles
Johnson, Ishmael Reed, and other novelists and writers who
debated all this. The key issue was whether writers like Ralph
Ellison and Albert Murray, who called us the omni-Americans,
were the good guys or the bad. Ishmael was arguing they're the
bad guys, because their faith was misplaced, that adhering to this
sense of inextricable Americanness, this aspiration, would be
rewarded. But if you decide that it's all just quixotic and misplaced, that leads to reactionary stuff.

◆ Finding a Balance

Both Loury and Kennedy now write occasionally for the
centrist-liberal *New Republic* (of which Loury is a contributing
editor), and both contributed to a special issue of the Democratic Leadership Council's (DLC) *New Democrat* magazine,
which Loury guest-edited, entitled "Shall We Overcome?" Kennedy couldn't agree more with Loury's comment about the reactionary consequences of succumbing to racialism, but Loury
is still wrestling with the costs and consequences of keeping
faith with the larger society. Some of that struggle surfaced in
a small-group discussion which both men attended at the invi-
tation of the Democratic Leadership Council, held in the base-
ment of Harvard's Robinson Hall in June 1996.

"There may not be as many fundamental clashes between
the black minority and the white majority as some think," said
the DLC's Will Marshall, posing the challenge,

but political alignments and strategies are congealed that way,
around the symbolism of an old civil rights consensus that's
breaking down. Can racial iconoclasts who've been marginalized
for telling that truth come together to create a safe harbor of support? We need to defend a civic culture that transcends group
identities. Can we find common ground in rebuilding the eco-

nomic basis of urban life with fewer race-specific initiatives, in normalizing life with more employment and homeownership?

Our challenge is to interrupt people going to their assigned spots on the floor every time some keyword like "preferences" is spoken. Conservatives say to liberals, "OK, you brought us in on the notion of color blindness, but now you want to change the debate with more racial classifications and remedies." Well, *we* don't want to change it that way, but neither do we see much color blindness coming from conservatives. How can we go to black leaders and say, "Stop pushing a strategy that's based on diminishing returns"?

Loury and Kennedy understood these questions only too well. They had come to Robinson Hall not to make any commitments to an organization whose own thinking was also in transition, but to talk with people who posed the right questions and had the will and, perhaps, the political connections to do something about them.

"There has to be clarity about motives," Loury responded, expressing his concern that race not be completely lost from the discussion.

> You talk about a new push on urban problems, and I agree it's needed, big-time. But when you debate why plants close as CEOs' incomes rise, or what to do about foreign competition, or whether to have more prisons or more midnight basketball, aren't there racial implications? Public figures on all sides of these issues who might want to discuss race rationally have strategic vulnerabilities which they try to mask by pointing at opponents who they claim would try to shoot them down if they brought up race at all.

Loury added that conservative whites do this as often as liberal blacks: When Jack Kemp dropped such defenses and "passed the 'motive test' with skeptical black leaders" by courting them with visions of small-business development and homeownership, "I heard talk in conservative circles that Jack had 'gone native.' "

"The worst thing is to let racists stampede us into *trying* to build a politics around their attacks," Marshall replied, trying to set out some limits on racial discourse.

> Politics can affect the answer if the question is, how do we get people out of a generation of poverty and the crime that comes with it? If affirmative action goes down and poverty goes up, the solution isn't to expand the welfare state, though it will take serious money to connect people to work and convert public housing subsidies to homeownership. The point is to convert paternalistic dollars to empowerment dollars.

Americans might support this, Marshall added, if more leaders, black and white, left and right, stopped accommodating and exploiting racial hustlers of all colors and persuasions: "People are tired of that. We're working with the counterintuitive notion that the country is getting ready for a new push on urban policy."

"But how many conservatives do pass the motive test on race?" Kennedy asked, worrying not just about how conservatives talk, but about whether they duck real problems that have a racial cast: "I don't sense that inner-city poverty gets Bill Kristol's blood running," he continued, referring to the Republican political strategist and editor of the *Weekly Standard*. "We need clarification about what we want. Before we talk about downplaying racial remedies, we need a clearer sense of what is racial justice and racial equality, and even what is integration"—a subject Kennedy had just addressed in the democratic-socialist quarterly *Dissent*. "Then we have to apply it to specific dilemmas," he concluded. Kennedy is no fan of race remedies; in a discussion of affirmative action in Michael Sandel's class, he called himself "a meritocratic fundamentalist." But he is decidedly a fan of thorough analysis, which smokes out racialist nonsense.

The Robinson Hall group reached no conclusions but agreed to meet again. Whether it does or not, the kind of discussion it held is indispensable to redeeming our otherwise arid, evasive public discourse on race. As a classical liberal moralist, Kennedy knows as well as conservatives that the soaring universalism of the old left tends to overreach and collapse into its most deadly antithesis, ethnic exoticism, as it has in Belgrade and Los Angeles. But Kennedy also knows that unbridled capitalism can divide and eviscerate civil society, driving some of the wounded into warring racial and ethnic camps. He finds little honest reckoning with this on either the left, which indulges the racial-identity trap, or the right, which indulges market and corporate excesses.

At the same time, ironically and less openly, the liberals flirt with free-market libertarianism and conservatives play with racial division. A seamless hypocrisy links both camps, which often deserve each other. While liberals, for example, are drawn to Loury as he calls for a national commitment to the urban poor, the depth of his concern for the casualties exposes all that is patronizing and ineffectual in others' moral posturing against racism. Loury would give race-consciousness more political room than Kennedy does, but he, too, draws the line whenever it threatens intellectual and civic integrity. As our politics and culture have weakened under the pressures of inner-city isolation and anomic consumerism, racist thinking has gained legitimacy among sophisticated liberals at the Ford Foundation, the *New York Times*, and in the Democratic Party, no less than it has among sophisticated conservatives at the American Enterprise Institute and the right-wing *American Spectator*, and in the Republican Party.

The best way to dissolve these hypocrisies is to reaffirm the two-tiered American civic faith the early civil rights movement mobilized so well. It synthesized parochial black religious communalism and strong universalism to strengthen an American civic culture, which, even in 1995, was still strong enough to induce one of its chief detractors, Louis Farrakhan, to hold his march on the Washington Mall. At its best, the American civic culture and civil religion have showed the world how to balance parochial loyalties with cosmopolitan opportunities and commitments. Now, after thirty years of flailing amid guilt and recrimination over the civic culture's old racial fault lines, it is time for the country to strike a new balance with its black citizens, who have been both its most fervent supporters and its most embittered assailants. The challenge has economic and political dimensions aplenty, but our purpose here is to ask what we can do culturally to vindicate individuals, of all colors, who want to affirm an American belonging that is not colored by others' racial prescriptions.

CHAPTER 7

WHAT WE HAVE LOST

◆ How One Civic Culture Worked

Since the late 1980s, the phrases "civic culture" and "civil society" have been tripping off the tongues of pundits and politicians, sad testimony to many Americans' growing sense that something awful is happening to the network of voluntary yet public associations upon which democratic government and a healthy economy depend. We're told that civic and social groups in which people learn to balance self-interest with communal teamwork—Little Leagues and bowling leagues, Boy Scouts and Girls Scouts, neighborhood improvement groups, churches, parent-teacher associations— are becoming shells of their former selves.

Economic and cultural upheavals are said to leave beleaguered citizens little time or disposition to join others in common endeavors, especially when "others" of even the same background treat one another like aliens. Gone, we're told, are the shared hopes and values that made cooperation possible and nourished individual dignity and fellow-feeling, even across ethnic and religious lines. Instead, people are withdrawing into atomized, defiantly selfish pursuits, or they are seeking a semblance of "belonging" in degraded sporting and musical spectacles or warring camps that are defined by little more than their hostility to one another.

Some of these alarums about civil society are excessive, especially when set against the riotous urban and frontier societies in our national past. But its deterioration is unmistakable, and, beyond speculating about the causes, we would do well to understand better how it worked, sometimes even to the benefit of "aliens" in its midst. One place to look is the long, conflicted relation to American civic culture of W.E.B. Du Bois, who bestrode black intellectual and political life from the post–Reconstruction era through the first crumblings of Jim Crow in the early 1960s, when he left this country to pursue a chimerical Pan-African, quasi-Marxist dream. Flawed though the Yankee New England civic culture of his youth was, it was sometimes brilliant at balancing parochial traditions and universal aspirations, individual autonomy and communal obligation. There is much to be learned from looking at Du Bois's encounters with it—and from his mistake in writing it off.

Born in Great Barrington, Massachusetts, in 1868—"by a golden river and in the shadow of two great hills, five years after the Emancipation Proclamation," as he put it portentously in his autobiography—Du Bois grew up in a traditional, Congregationalist civil society. Actually, there were several Yankee cultures, and in his remarkable life, Du Bois rang most of their chimes, soaring to contentious distinction among the Brahmins of Boston and mastering the Concord tradition of moralist dissent that ran from the early transcendentalism of Emerson and Thoreau through the abolitionism of Harriet Beecher Stowe and Horace Greeley. The western New England subculture of his youth was more democratic and less pietistic than those of Boston and Concord, more ironic and good-humored in its recognition of human failings, and more rational in its handling of them. As it happens, I grew up forty miles east of Du Bois and eighty years after him, and much of what he saw in Yankee New England was still palpable in the 1950s.

The civic culture of his youth carried on an intense moral

conversation with its natural environment. Of Great Barrington, Du Bois wrote:

> The town and its surroundings were a boy's paradise. There were
> mountains to climb and rivers to wade and swim; lakes to freeze
> and hills for coasting . . . and all of it was apparently property of
> the children of the town. My earlier contacts with playmates and
> other human beings were normal and pleasant. Sometimes there
> was a dearth of available playmates but that was peculiar to the
> conventions of the town where families were small and children
> must go to bed early and not loaf on the streets or congregate in
> miscellaneous crowds.

Similarly, the nineteenth-century New England cleric and re-
former Orestes Brownson observed:

> Our children are educated in the streets, by the influence of their
> associates, in the fields and on the hill sides, by the influences of
> surrounding scenery and overshadowing skies, in the bosom of
> the family, by the love and gentleness, or wrath and fretfulness
> of parents, by the passions or affections they see manifested, the
> conversations to which they listen, and above all the general pur-
> suits, habits and moral tone of the community.

Always, it seemed, a few leading citizens set the local moral
tone with "a bright, cheery courage despite some dryness and
gravity, a practical, insuppressible, active temperament with
the force of ten men, ready with a word for every emergency,"
as John Jay Chapman, a bearer of that tradition in the late
nineteenth century, characterized it. The best of these school-
teachers and officeholders taught their fellow citizens the arts
of civil discourse, almost on the sly, by example and without
too much preaching. Their deft wit and dauntless good cheer
deflected many a confrontation in classrooms, on playing
fields, and at town meetings.

Not everyone was genial, of course, but everyone was disciplined, and since one spoke up in a class or at a meeting only
after weighing one's needs respectfully against others', one's
well-chosen words carried more weight. One bore oneself in

ways that signaled a disciplined public-spiritedness and good-will, so one got the same in return. Self-important or self-absorbed body language was taboo; one rebuffed it in priggish moralists as well as in proles. Both individual and community were strengthened in these modest, mannered exchanges, not in psychodramas or litigation, certainly not in a conspicuously material, therapeutic, or otherwise "expressive" individualism.

This balance of individualism and community had a religious taproot, of course. Condemning Roman Catholic and Anglican priestly hierarchies, the Puritans who settled Massachusetts conceived a "priesthood of all believers," each one "justified" before God not by sacraments and the mass but by an intensely personal faith that emphasized introspection. Ministers instructed the faithful in the arts and limits of self-scrutiny, but individual moral vigilance was God's own instrument in building a New Jerusalem. By drawing the passions into a vortex of self-scrutiny, even the secular Yankee tradition of later years curbed gratuitous "communication," making few words say more because they were taken to issue from depths of private reckoning: "Good fences make good neighbors." "God helps those who help themselves." "Let your yea be yea, and your nay, nay." "Plain living and high thinking."

Du Bois was not a man of few words, yet he was marked by this tradition of reserved introspection:

In general thought and conduct, I became quite thoroughly New England. It was not good form in Great Barrington to express one's thought volubly, or to give way to excessive emotion. We were even sparing in our daily greetings. I am quite sure that in a less restrained and conventional atmosphere I should have easily learned to express my emotions with far greater and unrestrained intensity; but as it was I had the social heritage not only of a New England clan but Dutch taciturnity.

This was later reinforced and strengthened by inner withdrawals in the face of real and imagined discriminations. The result was that I was early thrown in upon myself . . . the habit of repression often returned to plague me in after years, for so early a habit could not easily be unlearned. The Negroes in the South, when I came to know them, could never understand why I did not naturally greet everyone I passed on the street or slap my friends on the back.

If the dominant Yankee culture was more rational than passional—and more tragic than perfectionist in its appreciation of human foibles—it was the more resilient for it. Once one internalized the rules of its road and learned how to "drive" in a way that respected other drivers' intentions and needs, one got more mileage out of civil discourse across lines of difference than one would have gotten by deconstructing the rules and leaving oneself and others with no trustworthy means of communication. New England civil society nourished more genuine public-spiritedness that way than do communities premised on intensely parochial or Promethean identities, or on sweepingly salvific or ideological systems—a paradox that needs explaining to some liberals, who forget how much social progress depends on accepting moral authority. When liberals view civil and cultural authority as inherently racist, for example, they only reinforce the expectation that blacks will live outside of civil society's strictures and rewards.

In Great Barrington, by contrast, Du Bois was a child of racial integration before the fact. Although there were fewer than fifty black families in his town of four thousand, he was set apart less by his color than by his quirky brilliance. His own family, descended on his mother's side from a Dutch settler's slave and the settler's own family, had lived in the area for more than a century before his birth. Du Bois's paternal grandfather, of mixed French Huguenot and black descent, passed for white at the elite Cheshire Academy and became something of a Victorian gentleman in New Bedford, from which many a Yankee slave ship had sailed. "He was not a 'Negro'; he was a man!" Du Bois wrote—a claim that might make more sense to a nineteenth-century New England Calvinist than to a late-twentieth-century liberal.

In Great Barrington, he said, "There was no real discrimination on account of color." Visiting his white friends' homes, he recalled,

> I think I probably surprised my hosts more than they me, for I was easily at home and perfectly happy and they looked to me just like ordinary people, while my brown face and frizzled hair must have seemed strange to them. Yet I was very much one of them. I was a center and sometimes the leader of the town gang of boys. We were noisy, but never very bad. . . . As time flew I felt not so much disowned and rejected as rather drawn up into higher spaces and made part of a mightier mission.

At his high school graduation in 1884, Du Bois, the only black in his class, was applauded repeatedly by an overwhelmingly white audience for an oration on the antislavery agitator Wendell Phillips, who had died that year and whose career prefigured Du Bois's in its opposition not only to racism but to capitalism. Frank Hosmer, the school's principal and a classic New England abolitionist, took up a collection among the town's white elite to send Du Bois to Fisk University in Tennessee. "The crusade of the New England schoolmarm was in full swing," Du Bois recalled later. "The freed slaves, if properly led, had a great future. . . . They needed trained leadership. I was sent to help furnish it."

Du Bois recalls that blacks in western Massachusetts spoke "an idiomatic New England tongue, with no African dialect. The [black] family customs were New England, and the sex mores," he wrote, perhaps a bit wistfully, as his father had abandoned him in infancy, causing him quiet consternation and shame in Calvinist, not racial, terms. "The color line was manifest, and yet not absolutely drawn," he wrote. "The racial angle was more clearly defined against the Irish than against me." Little in Du Bois's experience of race in Great Barrington prepared him for what he encountered in the South. If anything, his New England moralism must have deepened his shock when he went to Tennessee, still a teenager, a year after his graduation address in Great Barrington.

Du Bois's experience was anomalous, of course, even in abolitionist New England. And his biographer, David Levering Lewis, cautions that the great man's reminiscences about the region, by turns lyrical and vague, may have appropriated the best of the local civic culture when it suited him and rejected the rest when it reminded him of familial and social problems it didn't or couldn't help him resolve. Still, what we know of his early life deepens our understanding of race in America: Because the civic culture of his youth put so much weight on ethically autonomous yet publicly accountable individuals, it could liberate determined individualists from racial and even religious stereotypes. When respect for individualism is intense enough, its judgments of individuals are not so easily circumscribed by race.

◆ Calvinism and Capitalism

Because Yankee values emphasized how to get along as much if not more than they emphasized what to believe, they nourished, in some, a capacity for high-souled dissent strong enough to defy even established legal and economic constraints. New England's dissenters were most effective when, acting in the name of generally shared values, they credibly accused others of failing to honor them. One might search one's soul, commune with God through Bible, brooks, and trees, and then, like Bunyan's pilgrim, take one's stand against the dominant temporal powers. "The powers that be" is a resonant phrase because it reminds that they may *not* "be" tomorrow.

Steeped in this vaguely mystical civil religion, Du Bois opened a chapter in *The Souls of Black Folk* with the lines from the poet James Russell Lowell that expressed well its Protestant posture of righteous insurgency against established but corrupted temporal power:

Careless seems the great Avenger;
   History's lessons but record
One death-grapple in the darkness
   'Twixt old systems and the Word;

Truth forever on the scaffold,
    Wrong forever on the throne;
Yet that scaffold sways the future,
    And behind the dim unknown
Standeth God within the shadow
    Keeping watch above His own.

This is pure Yankee moralism. "For purposes of yeast, there was never such a leaven as the Puritan stock," wrote John Jay Chapman. Out of that "stock" and others that embraced its beliefs came the abolitionist crusade, the great pedagogical project that sent Du Bois and hundreds of New England schoolmarms to the South to "instruct" freed slaves, and a civil rights movement that combined black Baptist communalism with a race-transcendent, Calvinist theology of a personal responsibility and justification by a faith beyond color. Eventually Du Bois would claim that those values were too narrow for him and the world he encountered beyond. But he owed a lot to those values and he knew it. Because we are all legatees of this confluence of Protestant universalisms, many Southern whites, Northern reporters, and other firsthand witnesses were riveted and transformed by its emergence in the churches and on the streets of Montgomery, Birmingham, Selma, and Little Rock.

The biggest test of dissent in nineteenth-century New England was not racism but capitalism. Without "the Protestant ethic" of heroic individual striving, there would be no spirit of capitalism; yet without Protestant curbs on that capitalist spirit, the urgency of its accumulation and consumption would become idolatrous and self-destructive (as they are now). Without a strong religious faith, New England's aggressive, acquisitive economy could transmute individual initiative into greed, struggles for personal dignity into a kind of paranoia, and propriety into conformism.

Yankee civic culture never resolved this tension between its Calvinism and its capitalism. The Puritans' most prosperous descendants evaded it by construing material success as a sign of the grace of God, from Whom all blessings flowed. But consumption that was too conspicuous was blasphemous, so their pride in their plenty was masked by reserve. Asked by a nineteenth-century visitor to Boston where the ladies of Beacon Hill got their hats, a citizen retorted, "They don't *get* their hats; they *have* their hats," as if the goods had been bestowed, not bought. Actually, the hats came from an aggressive mercantile economy that was not above trading in slaves, penning up working girls in textile-mill towns, and pitting Irish-immigrant workers against "free" Northern blacks. One can only marvel at the iron restraints of faith and propriety that were needed to reconcile such an economy with its masters' priestly pretensions.

And yet the same restraints could be liberating, unleashing prodigious quantities of hard, productive work that tempered class differences in an apparent commonweal because work was understood as a form of divine service for rich and poor alike. While one awaited God's judgment, "plain living and high thinking" marked one's devotion, suffusing the industrious Yankee culture's norms of personal privacy, initiative, and propriety. For all the psychic strain those norms imposed, New Englanders not only didn't apologize for their way of life, they seldom explained it, and made understanding it an art: "They *have* their hats."

"Wealth had no particular lure," Du Bois recalls, even though "the shadow of wealth was about us. That river of my birth was golden because of the woolen and paper waste that soiled it. The gold was theirs, not ours; but the gleam and the glint was for all. To me it was all in order and I took it philosophically. I cordially despised the poor Irish and South Germans, who slaved in mills, and [I] annexed the rich and well-to-do as my natural companions. Of such is the kingdom of snobs!" This tension presaged the next century's hostilities between white-ethnic Catholics and blacks, when "race" would assume narrower meanings. But in Du Bois's time, blacks, even barred from Great Barrington's mills, were still so attached to what remained of yeoman farming and "service" industries that many of them affected to disdain mill work, as Du Bois did.

Moreover, industrial capitalism had not yet strained the town's civic culture to the breaking point. "Naturally the income was not proportioned to the effort," Du Bois wrote, "but we did not dream of a day when a man doing nothing could be a millionaire at thirty-five, while his fellow broke back and heart and starved." At the same time, something of Beacon Hill's moralism had penetrated Du Bois's Berkshires:

> I grew up in the midst of definite ideas as to wealth and poverty, work and charity. Wealth was the result of work and saving and the rich rightly inherited the earth. . . . I clearly came to understand that to be "on the town," the recipient of public charity, was the depth not only of misfortune but of a certain guilt. I presume some of my folk sank to that, but not to my knowledge. We earned our way.

In fact, Du Bois, after his father's abandonment, did support himself and his mother—earning his way at one time as Great Barrington's correspondent for the *Springfield Republican*, a beacon of the abolitionists in his time and my own hometown paper eighty years later. By the time I was a child, in the 1950s, Du Bois was assailing the class structure he had once accepted. Certainly, it had grown more severe. But it wasn't Great Barrington's hypocrisies about class that destroyed Du Bois's faith in Yankee civic culture. More likely, all that was wholesome in the village that raised this child left him so unprepared for what he found in the South that it seemed to have misled him about the world beyond its reach.

♦ Moralism Amok

The broader its reach, the more condescending New England's religious and civic moralism sometimes became: "The degradation of the black man did not cause [Ralph Waldo Emerson] sleepless nights (although he came to think better of the Negro's prospects, he apparently never lost a slight colorphobia)," writes Daniel Aaron of Emerson's reaction to abolitionism and the Civil War, "but the transformation of a man whatever his color into a 'thing' struck him as a profanation and a monstrous wrong. The moral dirt produced by slavery had to be cleaned up in order to make the United States inhabitable for the white man."

According to Van Wyck Brooks, the literary interpreter of Puritanism, when the jug of old New England finally cracked, spilling its Puritan wine, the liquid ran into the earth as rank commercialism, while the vapor and aroma rose heavenward in the dissociated mysticism of transcendentalism. Du Bois would complain bitterly that such high-souled dissent among the scions of New England's upper classes was driven mainly by guilt—that it deceived others and itself about how it had gotten its hats. Loftier reformers sometimes resorted to a purely gestural moralism as unrealistic about economic reality as were the older Puritan conventions it pretended to expose.

Despite such noble intentions, "the lower register of sensations and emotions which domesticate a man into fellowship with common life was weak," Chapman observed. Emerson, thinking of upper-class reformers, complained, "Young Americans are educated above the work of the times and the country, and disdain it. Many of the more acute minds pass into a lofty criticism, which only embitters their sensibility to evil and widens the feeling of hostility between them and the citizens at large." Du Bois would later be characterized somewhat that way by black critics, and no wonder: Reminiscing about his youth in Great Barrington, he remarked, "At times I almost pitied my pale companions, who were not of the Lord's anointed and who saw in their dreams no splendid quests of golden fleeces." *Anointed!* How New England!

Insufferable though it could be when turned in upon its own parlors and psyches, the New England conscience did move mountains. Yankee abolitionism and postwar educational missions to the South confirmed Chapman's assessment of the Puritan ability to enflame social movements. Of Harriet Beecher Stowe, whose *Uncle Tom's Cabin* almost displaced *The Pilgrim's Progress* as a moral primer before the Civil War, Vernon Parrington wrote: "A thinker who can dig from the harsh soil of Calvinism the doctrine of disinterested benevolence will discover a tender conscience in his own bosom." Of Horace Greeley, he wrote, "With his Yankee capacity for hard work, his daring enterprise, his vigorous independence, he embodied an extremely sensitive social conscience, keen sympathy for those who do the work of the world and a transparent honesty of mind and purpose."

So, too, it was with William Lloyd Garrison, William Cullen Bryant, Wendell Phillips, and other abolitionists. New England sent Bryant to the *New York Evening Post* and Greeley to the *New York Tribune* to remoralize public discourse in that city. It sent the Yankee schoolmarms to the South to instruct not only the freed slaves but, decades later, descendants of slaves such as C. Eric Lincoln, who recalls, in *Coming Through the Fire*, that, as a youth in Alabama in the early 1930s,

> I was fortunate enough to receive the best education available in the area, provided by dedicated New England spinsters who did not teach for money, but who bargained away their lives and their comfort out of a sense of *ought* that the "best people" of the South were unable to entertain.
>
> ... Such a prospect was patently unacceptable to the distressed prevailing Southern mind. ... The effective answer ... was to defang the threat of the Yankee education of Negroes by having the South itself do the educating. ... Nevertheless, there had been a significant crack in the holding pens of ignorance. ... At Trinity I read everything ... my delighted Yankee schoolmarms could import for me—Walter Scott, Shakespeare, Dryden, Pope, Goethe, Ovid, Pushkin ... Washington Irving, and the Transcendentalists.

The black sociologist E. Franklin Frazier would lampoon censorious Yankee missionaries as progenitors of an imitative, thin-blooded black bourgeoisie; C. Eric Lincoln, too, occasionally arches an eyebrow at them in his fiction. Yet, sixty years after his encounters with them, he could still recite to me his teachers' names and their New England hometowns.

As a student at Boston University, Martin Luther King, Jr., integrated a conservative New England theology into his black

Baptist communalism. There, too, a black student from Texas named Barbara Jordan steeped herself in New England's moral eloquence and transcended it. In 1973, as the House Judiciary Committee prepared to vote for Richard Nixon's impeachment, Representative Jordan told her colleagues and a national audience what she felt was at stake:

> I felt somehow for many years that George Washington and Alexander Hamilton just left me out by mistake. But through the process of amendment, interpretation and court decision I have finally been included in "We, the people." My faith in the Constitution is whole, it is complete, it is total, and I am not going to sit here and be an idle spectator to the diminution, the subversion, the destruction of the Constitution.

Here, as in the writings and speeches of Du Bois, King, and C. Eric Lincoln, a living black voice and a sepulchral voice of New England dissent become one.

It needn't matter whether a civic culture draws its nourishment from New England Calvinists' conscience-ridden individualism, from Southern black Baptists' passional communalism, from West Virginia coal miners' class-tinted folkways, from South Side Chicago's solid, working-class black traditions, or from any other distinctively American taproot. The question is whether a civic culture succeeds in balancing parochial traditions with universal aspirations, individual autonomy with communal obligation.

◆ Du Bois's Derailment

In Du Bois's case, the balance broke down. I have noted the suggestion that the more proper a "Victorian" he became, the more he was "educated above the work of the times and the country" and disdained it, passing into the "lofty criticism" that, in Emerson's description, "only embitters [one's] sensibility to evil and widens the feeling of hostility between [one] and the citizens at large." Du Bois also had to suppress

Calvinist shame at his own family's dissolution, which may have shadowed his assessments of the civic culture in which it occurred. In the end, New England may not have betrayed him as much as he rebuffed and transcended its inherent contradictions, for good reasons but with sad results.

Torn between the relative racial comity of his childhood and the racial moralism of his later years, he undertook star-crossed efforts to defeat racism with Pan-Africanism and replace colonialism with communism. The Du Bois whose early worldview was shaped by Calvinist moral rectitude understood well that there can be no humanist retreat from white racism into a black racialism that persists in treating racial differences as essential. Yet the Du Bois who fled his family's own tangled New England roots to confront the South's racial caste system and wrestle with nineteenth-century racial ideas could not bring himself to fashion an identity that wasn't essentially a reaction against white racism itself.

Writing about his subsequent withdrawal from America to Africa in 1961, he acknowledged that he had no primal or cultural tie to Africa that antedated white colonialism. "Since the fifteenth century these ancestors of mine and their other descendants have had a common history; have suffered a common disaster and have one long memory. . . . The real essence of this kinship is its social heritage of slavery, the discrimination and insults. . . ." Embittered by the West's soaring hypocrisy in this matter, he depicted a white racism so ubiquitous and implacable that it transmuted blackness into a fellowship with all nonwhites: ". . . and this heritage binds together not simply the children of Africa, but extends through yellow Asia and in to the South Seas. It is this unity that draws me to Africa."

This was a fatal mistake. Du Bois emigrated just as legal segregation was beginning to fall. The first American public announcement of his death in Accra two years later came to 250,000 people on August 28, 1963, at the March for Jobs and Freedom on the Washington Mall, an event that could not have contrasted more tellingly with the hideous state funeral staged by Ghana's Osagyefo ("Redeemer") Kwame Nkrumah.

In his *W. E. B. Du Bois*, David Levering Lewis describes the spectacle in Accra:

> Fellowship [at Du Bois's state-provided compound] gave way to a maximum-security autocracy in a wail of sirens and backfiring motorcycles as a behemoth Russian ZIL limousine arrived. (There were only three of these machines in the country—Nkrumah's, the Du Boises', and the Soviet ambassador's, whose country's gift they were.) The leader of Ghana, a trim, slight man with a polished forehead, descended briskly. . . .
>
> [The funeral was] intended to advertise abroad and to enhance at home, with solemnity and pageantry, the reality of an African nationhood still being consolidated. "O God, Our Help in Ages Past" filled the heated air as the trombones and tubas of the Central Army Band followed behind the ZIL and the slow-moving caisson. Next came two double columns of elite infantry in gold-braided tunics of crimson—rifle stocks reversed and cradled in underarm position—executing the distinctive, ceremonial glide, the famous Slow March, learned from British drillmasters. . . .
>
> During the next few days, the newspapers would tally the impressive cable traffic—from Gus Hall of the American Communist Party . . . to Kim Il Sung of North Korea. Walter Ulbricht of the now dismantled German Democratic Republic wished that "the memory of Dr. Du Bois—an outstanding fighter for the liberation and prosperity of Africans—[would] continue to live in our hearts." The cables from Mao Tse-tung and Cho En-lai were lengthy but less formulistic . . . reflecting the political and personal camaraderie that had been so much advertised during the Du Boises' two sojourns in China. . . . Expressing his sense of loss, [Soviet] premier Nikita Khrushchev wrote Shirley Graham that her husband's "shining memory" would stay forever "in the hearts of the Soviet people."

In the mid-1970s, C. Eric Lincoln visited Du Bois's grave in Accra. "It was overgrown, run-down, neglected. It was as if they'd forgotten all about him." But even more telling had been the funeral's Yankee hymn, the British Slow March, and the communist encomia. "It is Europe's fictions of Africa that we need to forget," Anthony Appiah writes. Du Bois's fictions, too. And even some of Alex Haley's.

◆ Civic Defaults

The obstacles to American civic renewal are too daunting for racialist solutions. A few years ago, Gladys Hernandez, an inner-city elementary school teacher in Hartford, Connecticut, sixty miles southeast of Great Barrington, took her students on a field trip. Half of them were African American; half were Puerto Rican, many of whom spoke little English; and virtually all were from poor, single-parent families. They were so isolated from the rest of the city, so bereft of the civic language and culture that helped Du Bois make sense of his youth along one of New England's "golden rivers," that the field trip was a revelation to Mrs. Hernandez as well as to the students. As she testified later in *Sheff v. O'Neill*, a 1993 case about inner-city school segregation, the students grew increasingly excited while riding along in the bus, because

> . . . it was like they had never seen a bridge. . . . The most extraordinary thing happened when they came to the river. They all stood up in a group and applauded and cheered, and I was aware that they were giving the river a standing ovation. And they were so happy to see the beauty of the river, something that most of us go back and forth [over] and never take time to look at. . . . [They] are sensitive to beauty and to their environment and the richness of the world, but so seldom do they have the opportunity to . . . encounter the world.

In an account of the case for *Harper's* magazine, James Traub wrote that "some of the trial testimony was so piercing that people wept in the courtroom." Reading Traub's account, I recalled the pleasure Du Bois had taken in his "boy's paradise" along the Housatonic, and my own pleasures growing up along the Connecticut River, just twenty miles north of Mrs. Hernandez's students. The *Sheff* trial transcript shows that Mrs. Hernandez had thought a lot about what her students had been missing. "How does the racial isolation and poverty concentration affect the self-esteem of your students?" the plaintiffs' lawyer asked. She replied:

Well, I think that children can overcome the stigma of poverty. I think that children can overcome the stigma of their ethnicity. But what they cannot overcome is the stigma of separation. That is like a "damned spot" in their being, in their self-image, a spot that, no matter what success you have, you can't wipe it out. . . . No amount of salary, money. . . . I wish I could go around and tell people that it hurts our children, that we're destroying our best resource.

Elsewhere in her testimony, Mrs. Hernandez acknowledges the importance of poverty and race, but here she points beyond them. What her students lacked was not only money, but also a civic culture like that described by Du Bois and Orestes Brownson—one that could inspire, discipline, and induct its youth into a larger social and natural world. Certainly that required money, and Mrs. Hernandez was not shy in saying so. But Traub found that Hartford, whose students are 92 percent nonwhite and 64 percent poor, spends more money per capita on them than does middle-class, suburban Glastonbury, where a school he visited sent most graduates to college even though it was *less* well-equipped than a sister school in the inner city. "The kids in Glastonbury were simply replicating their parents' success, as the kids in Hartford were on their way to replicating their parents' failure," Traub noted.

Their parents' failure—a phrase pregnant with judgments of the sort made also by Du Bois, but not by liberal racists for at least thirty years. "What about *justice*?" I can hear some liberals ask. "What would happen to blacks in a civic culture like the old one, in all its oppressive conformity?" The early civil rights movement had an answer old New England would have understood. Because the movement invoked moral judgments in order to convict white segregationists of sin, it was able to point them toward redemption. And its civic and moral standards did not exempt its own members, black as well as white, from criticism, even in the teeth of oppression. Ultimately, it understood that right and wrong have nothing to do with race.

Sometimes, what Gladys Hernandez called "the stigma of separation" seems partly self-imposed. "Yo, Mister Sleeper!" an unidentified young man accosted me in a voice mail message he left at the New York *Daily News*. "If you've got time to write about minister Farrakhan, why don't you take the time to write about why we like him?" My column that day had lamented that, at the previous day's Million Man March, so many rightfully angry, yearning, decent black men had gotten conned by Farrakhan, whose performance had puzzled and then bored even the few who had come primarily to hail him. My caller continued:

Why don't you write about how we were systematically taught to hate by white slave owners? Why didn't you talk about how we had to be in separate, distinct burial grounds because we weren't fit to be buried in the same ones with you?

You white people are so condescending. Minister Farrakhan is speaking the truth, but all you want to do is come out with your own hidden agenda. Your world is crashing under the weight of your own evil. This man is a power in this country. You white people are gonna have to accept that. The more you call him a liar, the more we love him. The more bad shit y'all say about him, the more we love him. You don't want to see him around? Then don't say anything about him.

But you know what? You white people are the reason so many people were at the rally yesterday. Don't you see that? You talk about Martin Luther King. Well, Martin Luther King is dead, and you killed him. You Jews and the U.S. Government were his enemies. . . . You killed him.

So you need to stop being such damned hypocrites. We're gonna grow great in spite of all that you do. We're getting stronger, while you're getting weaker. We're gonna rise up. You keep on doing the same thing you tried to do since this country was created, you're gonna fail like you're failing now.

The caller was right about the history of white hypocrisy and brutality, but his impulse to make me understand that history was more "all-American" than he may have known. He was wrestling, I think, with Du Bois's famous question: "Can I be both [an American and a Negro]? Or is it my duty to cease to be a Negro as soon as possible and to become an American?" Obsessed with defying history by pegging blacks' rise to an apocalyptic white fall, he was trapped shadowboxing with ghosts. By his own choice, *he* was a ghost, speaking his "truths" anonymously into a voice-mail receptor; so *I* became a ghost, too, unable to respond or even to tell him I had bothered to listen.

I figured him for around twenty years old, perhaps an undergraduate like many I'd met over the years. He protested separate burial grounds, but were his college alumni association to convene a meeting to plan a new, integrated cemetery, he would rise from his seat—at the back of the hall, of course—and protest, "You white people are trying to deny us our peoplehood in death, just as you've tried to deny it to us in life." Whatever his judgment about historical exclusions, he would never admit to wanting to share a burial ground with whites now. He was trapped between past and future, between a black separation and an American belonging.

It happens all the time: For want of a secure footing in a shared civil society, many blacks struggle aimlessly with Du Bois's unresolved question. *Los Angeles Times* columnist Karen Grigsby Bates warns white readers that even the most refined of their black colleagues at work may well vote for Marion Barry or Al Sharpton (as, indeed, blacks have done overwhelmingly in several elections) to "send a message." Yet, in another column, she finds it "insulting" that whites assume that "all blacks think alike." Maybe so, but if blacks give their votes overwhelmingly to leaders like Barry and Sharpton, something else rings true, as it did in the O. J. Simpson acquittal and the message on my voice mail: "The more bad shit y'all say about [the black villain of the day], the more we love him."

But then what? No one who sends such a message answers this question seriously. Racial "message" senders are tree shakers, not jelly makers; they think it their duty only to evoke and provoke, to spin black pain and anger into webs of narrative and metaphor—"We're gonna rise up. . . .

You're gonna fail. . . ." Someone else—always, someone else—will have to turn such sentiments into a viable politics and policy.

As we have seen, people like my caller can take their cues even from professors. In 1995, I was on a panel discussing ethnic differences in New York City when one panelist, J. Phillip Thompson, a black assistant professor of political science at Barnard, said, "People have to keep in mind that African-American attitudes toward property may vary, because we *were* property. We were *owned.*" It was the kind of showstopper that often prompts whites in an audience to shrink with shame—and sometimes seems calculated to make them do just that.

Sometimes they shouldn't and, this time, I didn't. "Well, then," I responded, parodying multicultural doctrine, "I guess you can't blame racism for prompting 77 percent of New York City's 'Asian' voters to back Rudolph Giuliani over David Dinkins in the 1993 mayoral election. Koreans run so many dry-cleaning and grocery stores in New York that obviously they don't confuse twentieth-century property ownership with the slave trade. But Dinkins failed to protect them when some Korean stores in Brooklyn were subjected to a long, extortionist 'boycott' by a small group of black militants. Although Koreans had backed Dinkins in 1989, they turned against him in 1993, so their political differences with the black community were rooted in culture, not racism."

"I don't even understand your point," Thompson replied testily. But if he believed in cultural diversity, he should have. The "Korean boycott," as the two-year-long conflict was known, reflected a breakdown in black civic culture. An activist named Sonny Carson had organized it to punish Korean merchants who, he claimed, had "an attitude" toward black customers and were out to "destroy" the local community's economy and culture. Yet the Korean stores provided the only late-night shopping and lighting in local commercial centers that usually shut down after dark, in fear of crime. What Carson and the boycotters really wanted was a piece of the profits: "We are going to take back our community by any means necessary," said Carson associate Cóltraine Chimurenga. He never mentioned the only "means" that would have worked: Recruit and train young blacks to work fifteen hours a day at low wages, in close family units, collecting, scrubbing, displaying and selling vegetables. Koreans do that in order to pay their debts to ethnic lending societies that pool the money to invest in the stores. They can do it because they have a culture in which people keep their families and their promises.

In contrast, consider an example of the power that is forfeited by those who always send "messages" and "fight the power." In 1960, J. Raymond Jones—a black politician who, instead of sending "messages," patiently built so strong a Democratic machine in Harlem that he became the Democratic Party leader of all Manhattan—drove a hard bargain with House Speaker Sam Rayburn in a hotel room at the party's national convention in Los Angeles. Rayburn needed delegate support for a presidential bid by his fellow Texan, Lyndon Johnson, so Jones got Rayburn to promise that if Manhattan's convention delegates backed Johnson over John F. Kennedy on the first ballot for the presidential nomination, Rayburn would make Harlem congressman Adam Clayton Powell chairman of the powerful House Education and Labor Committee, and Johnson would be a strong ally in the civil rights struggle.

Kennedy won the nomination, and Johnson had to settle for the vice presidency, at least for a while. But since Jones had kept his part of the bargain, Rayburn kept his. Alas, Powell squandered the power Jones had won for him by sending pointless, nose-thumbing "messages" to the crackers in Congress. He may have enjoyed himself, but others had to pick up the pieces. Jones was dismayed but not disillusioned. In 1990, at age ninety-one, he told me that many black politicians "view the media as an opponent" and prosecutors as out to get them, and he acknowledged they "are partially correct." But, he added, "the media is the enemy of all politicians, period. And it is up to politicians to set such a standard, and maintain it to such a high degree, that there will be nothing justifiable" in the inevitable exposés and probes. Still more important, Jones said, is marshalling votes and bargaining hard in politics, and, at the same time, starting businesses.

The late Commerce Secretary and Democratic National Committee Chairman Ronald Brown grew up in Jones's Harlem and was a product of such thinking. Brown struck many as an opportunist, but he became so powerful that he no longer had to "send" messages but could deliver them in person or, as often, receive and act on messages sent by others. This is a politics of impassioned gradualism, not utopian revolution. But while the Jones/Brown model of effective engagement with the larger society has its seamy, back-room deal-making side, there are other, even more constructive examples set by black writers, educators, activists, and political leaders.

For example, in Southern California, San Antonio, Chicago, Baltimore, and the New York metropolitan region, the Industrial Areas Foundation (IAF) has trained powerful civic organizations of working-poor residents of inner-city neighborhoods to gain substantial power by striking just the right balances between racial or ethnic affinity and color-blind civic virtue, and between personal responsibility and communal obligation. Grounded in coalitions of religious congregations that are often predominantly black or Hispanic, the IAF groups never wave racial or evangelical banners in their dealings with local political and economic elites; they go out of their way to include local white churches as they build affordable housing, set up schools, improve public services, and prompt city councils to pass "living wage" bills to help the employees of private companies doing work for local governments. IAF's two-tiered civic model, which I have portrayed in *The Closest of Strangers* and the journalist William Greider has described in his writings, is catching on among other groups; I wish it would catch on in Evelyn Hernandez's Hartford neighborhood. Yet it is barely comprehended by politicians, philanthropists, journalists and other social observers who insist on viewing public life through racial or ideological lenses.

Our purpose here isn't to examine such models but to challenge the racial mind-set that inhibits them when liberals kow-tow to racial message-senders, reinforcing the stigma of separation. Amid the color-coding and shadowboxing, liberals should train themselves to send some clear messages right back. To the "by any means necessary" crowd, they should say, as J. Raymond Jones probably would, "Put up or shut up." When I asked Jones what he thought of the Brooklyn black boycotters' claims that since other racial groups and mobs used force and fraud, they should, too, he responded:

> That's what they did say in my time, but it's an argument for people who don't think. We could proceed on that basis and wreck the market. When I went into the ice business, I simply did the same thing the Italian and Irish boys did. When they started invading my territory, I invaded theirs. I bought every piece of junk I could lay my hands on, filled it with ice, and went into their neighborhood. One day on 116th Street, I saw a mob getting together. [But] before it got messy, [Tammany Hall leader] Jimmy Hines pulled his people out and we got together and agreed simply to compete. I said, "We're not scared, we're not gonna run. If everybody is trying to take control and nobody has control, soon the cops will take control." Well, he understood what I was talking about.

Sonny Carson's demonstrators would have no such trouble competing legitimately with the Koreans. What do they lack that Jones did not, even in Depression-era Harlem? Suppose that the Koreans had actually closed their thirty-odd stores in black Brooklyn neighborhoods, as Carson demanded, and had told all their customers to go to Carson for vegetables. Could he have taken over and run all those stores? Yet who was stopping him and the other militants from opening up their own cooperatives, farmers' markets, or stores and urging local residents to "buy black"? It doesn't take much capital to start a greengrocery. If the business culture and work habits are there, the investors will be found. If the culture and habits aren't there—if, as Randall Kennedy noted, few who called one another "Brother" at the Million Man March would have been willing to "lend this Brother $100"—then it is wrong just to blame racism, let alone to invoke the days when blacks were other people's property.

That is the point most white liberals seem not to understand or acknowledge. In Jones' view, only a racist would characterize the boycotters as victims of racism. And doing that would only compound racism by refusing to pay the demonstrators the compliment of holding them to elementary standards of market competition, political and economic organizing, and civil discourse. To trade on the "We were property" argument is to deny Jones's and the IAF groups' achievements and to insult most blacks, who don't trade on victimization and were embarrassed by the boycott rhetoric, even if somewhat cowed by it.

So the importance of civic culture cannot be overemphasized. When the disadvantaged lack clear moral signals and the footholds that come with them, racial and other divisions run riot, as they did in Los Angeles (which has no civic culture) after the acquittals of the police officers who had beaten Rodney King. Instead of mobilizing a disciplined, well-focused anger, political leaders who had promoted racial division watched helplessly as it dissolved into a war of all against all. Romantically or opportunistically, black leaders such as Representative Maxine Waters tried to call the riot an "uprising." It was really social dissolution, lacking the outraged dignity that would have come from a social moral center. Poor people desperately need such grounding. Liberals who think that it cannot be had until racism and poverty have been abolished should check their assumptions with Nelson Mandela, or, for that matter, with Malcolm X or Karl Marx.

When 149 garment workers met their deaths in 1911 at New York City's Triangle Shirtwaist Company in a fire caused by the owners' negligence and greed, a disciplined, cohesive union—grounded in a Jewish subculture that had to transcend itself with universal appeals because the owners, too,

were Jewish—sidelined the would-be bomb-throwers in its
midst and mounted a great, silent march whose civic discipline moved the city and drove legislation and economic justice. It was a vast improvement over New Yorkers' reactions to
rich draft-dodgers and poor blacks during the Civil War, when
rioting and anarchy drove the novelist Herman Melville to his
Manhattan rooftop, where he conceived this lament for civil
society's eclipse:

> All civil charms and priestly spells
> That late held hearts in awe;
> Fear bound, and subject to a better sway
> Than sway of self; these like a dream dissolve,
> And man rebounds whole aeons back in Nature.

Liberals should stop flirting with such decadence in the name
of "rights," and they should rediscover civil charms. Taking a
leaf from Du Bois's New England, they should stop conflating
moral obligation with repression when, in fact, it is often
empowering.

The evidence of American liberalism's sad recent history—
and, for that matter, of the even sadder "revolutions" abroad
in our time—shows that overthrowing civic cultures (or turning one's back on them, as Du Bois did) for the sake of tribal
liberations or universalist abstractions wins not more justice
but, literally, more death. Counting bodies is not a bad rule of
thumb to use when assessing the apparently thrilling alterna-
tives to the impassioned gradualism of the New England civic
culture and the pragmatism of a J. Raymond Jones. Instead
of threatening to get somewhere "by any means necessary,"
insurgents, both left and right, black and white, should
find ways to affirm civic culture's strengths and redeem its
flaws.

The problem is not that economic exploitation, racism, and
cultural oppression don't exist. It is that liberal racism like
Derrick Bell's and Andrew Hacker's made it harder to nurture
moral and civic standards that undercut racism and strength-
en movements against obvious injustice. "This was the gift of

New England to the freed Negro: not alms, but a friend; not cash but character," Du Bois wrote. It is a gift he shouldn't have discounted, and it is the most important gift liberals can make to the racial shadow-boxers they now so wrongly indulge.

CHAPTER 8

A COUNTRY BEYOND RACE

"The problem of the twentieth century is the problem of the color line," Du Bois wrote in 1903, challenging but perpetuating the nineteenth-century notion that race differences are so profound that one's skin color determines one's destiny. That makes even less sense now than it did then, and America will make no sense at all in the years ahead unless it fulfills its destiny to become a society beyond race. Standing now as close to the next century as Du Bois did to the last when he penned his grim prophecy, we must speak a new truth: The problem of the twenty-first century is the challenge of racelessness, of the color line's complete dissolution.

We have seen that liberals, instead of welcoming that prospect and helping the country to cope well with its consequences, are clinging to color with a desperation as puzzling as it is unseemly. In the name of "diversity"—but in deference to race hustlers, ideologues, and opportunists—liberals are chasing phantasms of racial difference, shrinking from the new America that is unfolding before our eyes. Racism endures, of course, and it is duplicitous and cruel; that only makes liberals' own complicity in it all the more fateful and unforgivable.

The stakes are uniquely American, but, ultimately, they are global. None of the battlefield campfires dotting the globe in the new century's early dawn illumines a color line. Hutus against Tutsis, English against Irish, Iraqis against Kurds, Serbians against Bosnians, Pakistanis against Indians, Russians against Chechnyans, even Jewish against Muslim Semites in the Middle East—in each of these conflicts, the opponents are racially indistinguishable. Their differences turn on religion, language, or ideology and cannot be comprehended by race, much less by a "multicultural" education that equates having a skin color with having a culture.

Why have American liberals gotten this so wrong? "Multiculturalism is the price America is paying for its inability or unwillingness to incorporate into its society African-Americans [as] it has incorporated so many groups," writes the sociologist Nathan Glazer. He is all too painfully right. But pedagogy that conflates cultures with colors exacts far too high a price. Liberals are rightly suspicious of conservatives who assail multiculturalism in the name of a transracial America they did precious little to open to blacks, but that suspicion cannot justify liberals' fatalistic acceptance of the racialist shams in our classrooms, courtrooms, workplaces, and election districts.

The air inside the edifice of liberal racism is growing stale, and it is scented with death. The inhabitants of that edifice are discovering that racial narratives do not cultivate democratic predispositions, that Ebonics and much of what passes for bilingualism do not enrich civic dialogue, and that racial multiculturalism offers nothing to mixed-race children and others who want to escape their immigrant or racial corrals. Racial narrators who deny that reading dead white males such as Thoreau and Whitman can stimulate young blacks now as it did Richard Wright and Ralph Ellison are really denying that black kids can be taught to read the American literature that is their precious heritage, too. Some multiculturalist pedagogues want not the "inclusion" they claim to seek but a ritual certification of exclusion that garners them paychecks, moral cachet, and sometimes even opportunities to exploit others of the same color in the name of race loyalty. Let us break up these games and break out of the building.

The philosopher Alasdair MacIntyre has noted that people are "storytelling animals" who become "possessed" by the stories that orient them in the world. But while every racial, ethnic, and religious group considers its own narrative of oppression, assertion, and redemption unique, most follow familiar patterns of self-definition, self-maintenance, and contention with others. Anticipating such patterns, constitutional framers such as James Madison created a system that requires "secular rationality as a basis for communication," relegates religions and philosophies to the private sphere, and yet suffuses the body politic with enough Judeo-Christian universalism to give it a moral mission.

With each of these commitments now openly challenged, America is in crisis. Since even the old elites lack coherent narratives, black marginality has become less exceptional and more typical of the whole country's problem. But merely enlarging the collection of group grievances and accusatory narratives only strengthens the allure of separatism. As I asserted at the outset, precisely because the United States is becoming more racially, ethnically, and religiously complex, liberals should be working overtime to identify and nurture at least a few shared national principles and bonds that deepen a sense of common belonging and nourish democratic dispositions.

We need not proclaim a single new national "story" such as manifest destiny or leadership of the free world. "The reality of diversity in a civil society . . . makes clear that free people have the right and the obligation to choose their levels and kinds of commitments and the measures they might borrow from other groups or, through barter, might extend to them," writes the religious historian Martin Marty. Neither superpatriotism nor racial multiculturalism can fulfill this right and obligation. Nor can ideological understandings of power and wealth, as this bloody century has shown. We do need to rededicate our pedagogy and politics to the kind of civic culture that balances parochialism and universalism, individual responsibility and communal obligation, in everyday actions that yield real opportunities.

How to do it? Nurturing a cultural authority that draws from both the parochial and the universal and that is grounded in personal responsibility, not group grievances, is an art—perhaps, ultimately, a religious art, as the Industrial Areas Foundation groups demonstrate so well. All I can contribute here is a warning: The loss of a common narrative and consensual rites of passage is driving young people to cults, white militias, and ghetto gangs, and yearnings like theirs are running deep and gathering force. Searching for firmer common ground, Marty offers the philosopher Michael Oakeshott's conception of a "civil association" of communities that, like porcupines in winter, huddle for warmth yet keep some distance from each other's sharp quills. Humans cannot strike such a balance by instinct alone, however, and we need to pay closer attention to past attempts at social integration, as we did in the preceding chapter, and to cultivate more deliberately some common American sentiments and affections. That, not the politics of "difference," should preoccupy us now.

Alan Ehrenhalt showed powerfully in *The Lost City* that if we want the much-touted benefits of "community," we must accept a degree of conformity. To strengthen any social value, we must deepen the stigma against anyone who violates it. Liberals rightly stigmatize those who exclude others by race or sex. But terms of *inclusion* must also be specified in other ways and, yes, enforced. This liberals seldom do well. To invoke rights without responsibilities is to increase the damage being done to a community's moral tone by people who should be stigmatized as individuals, whatever their group label. As Glenn Loury and Randall Kennedy insist, society has an obligation to set and enforce basic standards and to punish their violation with stigma and shame, not in order to keep the historically disadvantaged down, but, if the judgments are sound, to give them firm moral footholds on the way to more freedom and power.

Out of a commitment to shared civic standards, we can find it in ourselves to give greater voice to what former senator Bill Bradley said to troublemaking black kids on city streets; to what the Bronx baker Peter Medona said to Andrew Hacker about those "troublemakers"; to what white Southern voters "said" to voting rights activists in the 1996 elections; to what Gay Talese said to the *Times*; to what Glenn Loury said to his liberal conference audience; and to what Randall Kennedy said to critical race theorists. And journalists can shuck off the mind-sets that screen out truth-tellers like these. When self-appointed racial spokespersons try to "send a message," we should all send this message back: "You do not have to act as powerless as you think you are. And you do not have to be so defiantly separate from the rest of us."

The millions of Americans who have no recoverable racial or ethnic identities can't reconvene or mobilize along the old lines that separated our forebears. The coordinates of those past struggles are gone, along with their angels and demons. The writer Richard Rodriguez says there ought to be a bumper sticker that reads: "Assimilation Happens." He's right. We cannot do without parochial loyalties and religious revivals, but they alone cannot sustain a decent balance of discipline and freedom. Nor, certainly, can bureaucratic government. And while markets have the virtue of throwing people together across old lines of division, markets cannot nourish virtue, either. At the very least, we should work harder to shake the false notion, propagated by the foundations and the media, that we would have little to give one another if color had no more cultural value than aesthetic preferences for brown or green eyes. "*Race is a fantasy*," writes C. Eric Lincoln. "A chimera. A stalking horse for power and privilege." People who know this and are trying to live beyond race deserve more support than they get now from politicians, the media, and the schools. A lot depends on the courage and good sense of those of us who not only won't be corralled by color-coders, patronized by guilt-mongers, or stampeded by race hustlers but will stand up to and *answer* them. Our strength resides not in more racial monitoring and tinny celebrations of "diversity" but in the gossamer threads and race-less glue of an endless American belonging which new leaders and artists among us will have to evoke.

In his essay "On Becoming an American Writer," James A. McPherson has written tellingly about his experience of the

struggle to achieve and sustain civic balance. A native of segregated Savannah, he felt and worked his way in the 1960s and
'70s toward an American belonging that transcends racism
and race itself. As he and others of his background pro-
gressed, they found themselves

> trying to make sense of the growing diversity of friendships [and]
> increasing familiarity with the various political areas of the country.
> We never wanted to be "white," but we never wanted to be
> "black," either. And back during that period [of the late 1960s]
> there was a feeling that we could be whatever we wanted. But, we
> discovered, unless we joined a group, subscribed to some ide-
> ology, accepted some provisional identity, there was no contrac-
> tual process for defining and stabilizing what it was we wanted to
> be. We also found that this was an individual problem, and in
> order to confront it one had to go inside one's self.

"Going inside one's self" is precisely what liberal racists of all
colors fear to do. They flee such self-scrutiny by shouting
about "our people" and "sending a message." No wonder that
Loury entitled a 1994 book of his essays criticizing liberal
racism *One By One from the Inside Out*. That is how a lot of
our work will have to be done. As McPherson envisions that
project,

> . . . each United States citizen would attempt to approximate the
> ideals of the nation, be on at least conversant terms with all its
> diversity, carry the mainstream of the culture inside himself. As
> an American, by trying to wear these clothes he would be a syn-
> thesis of high and low, black and white, city and country, provin-
> cial and universal. If he could live with these contradictions, he
> would be simply a representative American.
> . . . [This status] can be achieved with or without intermarriage,
> but it will cost a great many mistakes and a lot of pain. It is, finally,
> a product of culture and not of race. And achieving it will require
> that one be conscious of America's culture and the complexity of
> all its people. . . . Such a perspective would provide a minefield of
> delicious ironies. Why, for example, should black Americans
> raised in Southern culture not find that some of their responses

are geared to [white] country music? How else . . . am I to account for a white friend in Boston who taught me much of what I know about black American music? . . . Most of us are products of much more complex cultural influences than we suppose.

As blacks like McPherson disown whatever is comforting in racial soothsayers like Farrakhan, whites must disown something comforting, too. Because we long excluded blacks from society's subtlest corruptions and most basic opportunities, we have often expected blacks to come into public life as bearers not only of rebukes and rebellions but also of a kind of salvation, a reservoir of special feeling and perception tapped in black music and the searing moral force of a Martin Luther King, Jr.

Of both burdens, blacks have borne more than enough. For all its wrong turns and dead ends, the black quest for American acknowledgment and belonging is the most powerful epic of unrequited love in the history of the world. Even if every broken heart could be mended and every theft of opportunity redressed, there would, of course, remain a black community of memory, loss, and endurance. And so there should. But ultimately there can be only transcendence—an American becoming, without parallel, without equal. Pending that, nothing is more un-becoming than a sentimental, guilt-hobbled white liberalism.

"The old strategies of accusation, isolation, and containment have broken down," writes C. Eric Lincoln, who has found in his own deep experiences of racism the springs of a transracial vision. "The supreme disloyalty is not to a bell [of racial solidarity] that has tolled itself into silence, but to the bell that has yet to ring. . . . If transracial marriage is here, and biracial children are here, can transracial adoptions be far behind? . . . It is time now to reach for the hand that is reaching for tomorrow, whatever color that hand may be. The evening of today is already far spent."

To watch nonwhite Americans settling down to the ordinary business of running municipalities, military units, media, manufacturing, and money markets is to watch the angels of

blackness withdraw with the demons. It is to surrender condescension along with contempt. For all of us, it is to acknowledge that this country's redemption has not and will not come
through making race the organizing principle of our polity
and civic culture. Liberals must lead struggles against discrimination and abuse. But for those struggles to succeed, in all
other endeavors liberals must let race go.

WORKS CITED

Aaron, Daniel. 1973. *The Unwritten War: American Writers and the Civil War*. New York: Alfred A. Knopf.

————. 1994. *American Notes: Selected Essays*. Boston: Northeastern University Press.

Appiah, Anthony. 1992. *In My Father's House: Africa in the Philosophy of Culture*. New York: Oxford University Press.

Cash, W. J. 1992. (Published originally in 1941.) *The Mind of the South*. Oxford: University of Mississippi Press.

Cose, Ellis. 1997. *Color-Blind: Seeing Beyond Race in a Race-Obsessed World*. New York: HarperCollins.

Crouch, Stanley. 1995. *The All-American Skin Game, or, the Decoy of Race*. New York: Pantheon Books.

Cruse, Harold. 1987. *Plural But Equal: A Critical Study of Blacks and Minorities in America's Plural Society*. New York: William Morrow.

DeMott, Benjamin. 1996. *The Trouble with Friendship: Why Americans Can't Think Straight About Race*. New York: Atlantic Monthly Press.

Du Bois, W. E. B. 1989. *The Souls of Black Folk*. New York: Bantam. (Published originally in 1903.) Du Bois's reminiscences about growing up in Great Barrington and his recollections of his youthful attitudes toward wealth and welfare are taken from three autobiographical works, excerpted in *The Berkshire Reader: Writings from New England's Secluded Paradise* (Richard Nunley, editor,

Stockbridge, Massachusetts: Berkshire House Publishers, 1992.) The excerpted works by Du Bois are: *Darkwater* (New York: Harcourt, Brace, 1921); *Autobiography* (New York: International Publishers, 1968); and *Dusk of Dawn* (New York: Harcourt, Brace, 1940).

Early, Gerald. 1995. "Understanding Afrocentrism," *Civilization*, July/August.

Emerson, Ralph Waldo. 1981. "Politics," in *The Portable Emerson*. New York: Viking Penguin.

Garrow, David. 1986. *Bearing the Cross: Martin Luther King, Jr. and the Southern Christian Leadership Conference*. New York: William Morrow.

Glazer, Nathan. 1997. *We Are All Multiculturalists Now*. Cambridge: Harvard University Press.

Hacker, Andrew. 1992. *Two Nations: Separate, Hostile, and Unequal*. New York: Scribner.

Haley, Alex. 1976. *Roots*. New York: Doubleday.

Harris, Eddy L. 1992. *Native Stranger: A Black American's Journey into the Heart of Africa*. New York: Simon & Schuster.

Kennedy, Randall. 1989. "Racial Critiques of Legal Academia," *Harvard Law Review*, No. 102.

————. 1997. *Race, Crime, and the Law*: New York: Pantheon. Kennedy's Lionel Trilling Lecture has been published as "My Race Problem—And Ours," *The Atlantic*, May, 1997.

Lasch, Christopher. 1991. *The True and Only Heaven: Progress and Its Critics*. New York: W. W. Norton.

Lewis, David Levering. 1993. *W. E. B. Du Bois: Biography of a Race, Vol. 1 (1868–1919)*. New York: Henry Holt.

Lincoln, C. Eric. 1996. *Coming Through the Fire: Surviving Race and Place in America*. Durham, N.C.: Duke University Press.

Loury, Glenn. 1992. *One By One from the Inside Out: Essays and Reviews on Race and Responsibility in America*. New York: Free Press.

McPherson, James Alan. 1978. "On Becoming an American Writer," *The Atlantic Monthly*, December.

————. 1993. "Junior and John Doe," in *Lure and Loathing*, Gerald Early, ed. New York: Viking Penguin.

Marty, Martin E. 1997. *The One and the Many: America's Struggle for the Common Good*. Cambridge: Harvard University Press.

Nachman, Larry. 1993. "Black and White," in *Salmagundi*, Spring-Summer. For other critical reviews of Andrew Hacker's *Two Na-*

tions, see David Brion Davis, "The American Dilemma," in *New York Review of Books*, July 16, 1992; Glenn Loury, "Liberal Racism," in *One by One from the Inside Out*; and Alan Wolfe, "The New American Dilemma," *The New Republic*, April 13, 1992.

Parrington, Vernon L. 1927. *Main Currents in American Thought, Vol. 2: The Romantic Revolution in America, 1800–1860*. New York: Harcourt, Brace.

Raines, Howell. 1983. *My Soul Is Rested: The Story of the Civil Rights Movement in the Deep South*. New York: Penguin Books.

Richburg, Keith. 1995. "Continental Divide," *Washington Post Sunday Magazine*, March 26.

———. 1997. *Out of America: A Black Man Confronts Africa*. New York: Basic/New Republic Books.

Steele, Shelby. 1990. *The Content of Our Character*. New York: St. Martin's Press.

Talese, Gay. 1969. *The Kingdom and the Power*. New York: World Publishing Co.

Thernstrom, Abigail. 1987. *Whose Votes Count? Affirmative Action and Minority Voting Rights*. Cambridge: Harvard University Press.

Traub, James. 1994. "Can Separate Be Equal?" *Harper's Magazine*, June.

Wilson, William Julius. 1996. *When Work Disappears: The World of the New Urban Poor*. New York: Alfred A. Knopf.

Wolfe, Alan. 1996. *Marginalized in the Middle*. Chicago: University of Chicago Press.

INDEX

FOR THE BEST IN PAPERBACKS, LOOK FOR THE

In every corner of the world, on every subject under the sun, Penguin represents quality and variety—the very best in publishing today.

For complete information about books available from Penguin—including Puffins, Penguin Classics, and Arkana—and how to order them, write to us at the appropriate address below. Please note that for copyright reasons the selection of books varies from country to country.

In the United Kingdom: Please write to *Dept. JC, Penguin Books Ltd, FREEPOST, West Drayton, Middlesex UB7 0BR.*

If you have any difficulty in obtaining a title, please send your order with the correct money, plus ten percent for postage and packaging, to *P.O. Box No. 11, West Drayton, Middlesex UB7 0BR*

In the United States: Please write to *Consumer Sales, Penguin USA, P.O. Box 999, Dept. 17109, Bergenfield, New Jersey 07621-0120.* VISA and MasterCard holders call 1-800-253-6476 to order all Penguin titles

In Canada: Please write to *Penguin Books Canada Ltd, 10 Alcorn Avenue, Suite 300, Toronto, Ontario M4V 3B2*

In Australia: Please write to *Penguin Books Australia Ltd, P.O. Box 257, Ringwood, Victoria 3134*

In New Zealand: Please write to *Penguin Books (NZ) Ltd, Private Bag 102902, North Shore Mail Centre, Auckland 10*

In India: Please write to *Penguin Books India Pvt Ltd, 706 Eros Apartments, 56 Nehru Place, New Delhi 110 019*

In the Netherlands: Please write to *Penguin Books Netherlands bv, Postbus 3507, NL-1001 AH Amsterdam*

In Germany: Please write to *Penguin Books Deutschland GmbH, Metzlerstrasse 26, 60594 Frankfurt am Main*

In Spain: Please write to *Penguin Books S. A., Bravo Murillo 19, 1° B, 28015 Madrid*

In Italy: Please write to *Penguin Italia s.r.l., Via Felice Casati 20, I-20124 Milano*

In France: Please write to *Penguin France S. A., 17 rue Lejeune, F-31000 Toulouse*

In Japan: Please write to *Penguin Books Japan, Ishikiribashi Building, 2-5-4, Suido, Bunkyo-ku, Tokyo 112*

In Greece: Please write to *Penguin Hellas Ltd, Dimocritou 3, GR-106 71 Athens*

In South Africa: Please write to *Longman Penguin Southern Africa (Pty) Ltd, Private Bag X08, Bertsham 2013*